God Bless you,

Myron Floren

Accordion
Man

ACCORDION MAN

Myron Floren and Randee Floren
with a Foreword by Lawrence Welk

 THE STEPHEN GREENE PRESS
Brattleboro, Vermont

Produced in the United States of America.

Designed by Bywater Production Services.

Published by The Stephen Greene Press, Fessenden Road, Brattleboro, Vermont
05301.

Library of Congress Cataloging in Publication Data
Floren, Myron.
  Accordion man.

  1. Floren, Myron.   2. Accordionists—United States—
Biography. I. Floren, Randee.   II. Title.
ML419.F62A3   786.9'7 [B]   81–6583
ISBN 0–8289–0400–6   AACR2

To Berdyne

Contents

Preface

Over half my life has been spent as a member of the Champagne Music Makers, but I had many experiences as a traveling musician before I joined Lawrence Welk and became a part of his family. I want to share what happened with you. It will come as no surprise that through the years I have had some serious problems; perhaps my way of dealing with them may in some small way help and encourage others with similar difficulties. My life has been touched by millions of wonderful people who, I hope, have gained just half as much from me as I have from them. This book is for all of you.

When Bill Eastman of The Stephen Greene Press approached me about writing my autobiography, I felt flattered and honored that he thought there might be enough interest in my life to warrant the time and expense needed to put such a book together. In the end, my wife and I started putting some thoughts on paper, and after we did some soul searching, these pages began to take shape.

Music has been very good to me. I have been blessed with an understanding and loving wife, Berdyne. She is more dear to me now than she was the day we married. Together we have had five beautiful daughters: Randee Lee, Kristie Ann, Robin Gay, Holly Jean, and Heidi Lynne.

Thanks to my daughters, I have "sons" now too: Jack McCooey, married to Randee; Bob Burgess, married to Kristie; Sam Gennawey, married to Heidi; and Tom Cippola, married to Robin. And last, but surely not least, I have two wonderful grandchildren, Becki Jane and Robert Floren Burgess.

For over thirty years Lawrence Welk has been my boss and friend. I'm looking forward to the next thirty.

I'm thankful to God that He has allowed me to live an active and rewarding life. I'm also thankful for the people that I work with—everyone is special to me in a different way.

More than anything, I am grateful to God for my family, parents, and the millions of friends I have made over the years through the TV show and personal appearances.

Foreword

Myron Floren has been with me for over thirty years, and in all that time I have never known him to lose his temper—not even once. He stays so calm, serene, and good-humored in the midst of this temperamental television business that sometimes he doesn't seem human! Well, yes, of course he does—Myron is the most human of men. He's also one of the finest—completely honest, reliable, and so kind and understanding, we all love him. No wonder I keep trying to imitate him.

He and I have a great deal in common. Both of us grew up on farms in the Midwest. Both of us loved music—and dreaded becoming farmers. And both of us heard concerts by professional musicians, when we were in our teens, that convinced us we should become musicians too.

In my own case, a traveling accordionist named Tom Gutenberg came to our little town of Strasburg, North Dakota, and when I heard him play, I knew that's what I wanted to do with my life. And when Myron was a teen-ager, my little band and I played for a dance in his home-town of Webster, South Dakota, and he tells me when he heard us, he knew that's what he wanted to do too. (I tell him that when he saw us having so much fun on stage, he figured it was a great way to make a living, and he'd better get in on it fast!)

Well, as the world knows, Myron did become a master accordionist, and when I found him in 1950, I hired him immediately. My manager, Sam Lutz, nearly had a heart attack. "Are you crazy?" he spluttered. "Why would you want to hire an accordion player who plays better than you do?"

My answer to him then was the same as it would be now. All my life I have searched for the very best—in people, in performers, and in perfection of character. In Myron Floren, I found all three.

He has been invaluable to me, assisting in the directing of the orchestra and taking over management of a myriad of details whenever we go on tour. He is a real inspiration to all of us, as I'm sure his life story will be to you.

Lawrence Welk

Accordion
Man

Heerlen

Heerlen, the Netherlands.

Sunday, December 31, 1944. In sixty minutes the New Year would begin.

Suddenly I realized how bone tired I felt. So much had happened during the past six months, as I had journeyed from my familiar bed in Sioux Falls, South Dakota, to more than a hundred other beds, none of them comfortable, across Europe.

The soldiers who earlier had been entertained by our little USO troupe of five performers would celebrate the New Year as best they could under the circumstances.* But all I was interested in at that moment was getting some sleep. We had done five shows that day, all in a captured German ammunition bunker three stories underground. Over three hundred soldiers had been packed into the bunker for each show.

Their loud applause and laughter still rang in my ears. It had been a good day's work, and I hoped we had brought some relief from the tension and fear they had to endure. These front-line infantrymen had no way of knowing what the next few days, or even hours, held for them. Who could

*United Service Organization

1

tell how many would return to their families and loved ones crippled for life, or worse—in a flag-draped casket?

As I drifted off to sleep, a dream took me back to the farm. Pa and I were harvesting wheat on the West Forty. I was driving the old Fordson tractor, and he was riding the binder.

Suddenly the familiar sound of the tractor's engine was drowned out by the angry buzzing of bees from a hive we had accidentally disturbed. In seconds they were attacking me. There were too many to brush away.

Trying to escape, I was distracted by the sound of an airplane overhead. I looked up to spot it and found myself back in Heerlen, staring at the ceiling of my room in the little Dutch hostel in which our USO group was staying.

Still half-asleep, I glanced at my friend and fellow entertainer Don Rice, in the bed next to mine, and was amazed that he was still asleep. Why hadn't the bees wakened him too? I settled back on my pillow to let the monotonous engine drone of an airplane, somewhere overhead, lull me back to sleep.

Suddenly a change in the rhythm of the engine noise jerked me wide awake. It was the ear-splitting scream of a German Stuka bomber in a power dive—heading straight for us, I was sure! We were on the top floor of the hostel, with no place to hide. As I have heard Lawrence Welk say many times, years later, I thought, "Maybe I should have stayed on the farm!"

The shock of the explosion threw me out of my bed and across the room. I landed right under Don's bed (by this time he was also wide awake). He looked at me. "What was that?" he stammered in a voice barely above a whisper.

"It was a bomb," I answered. Then Don grinned and said, "I've heard of critics, but this is ridiculous!"

Some plaster had fallen from the ceiling, and pictures

2

were knocked off the walls, but we were unhurt. The pounding of antiaircraft guns and bombs could be heard in the distance. People were running and shouting in the streets below. Ambulances were screaming all over the city. Then a horrible thought hit me: "My accordion!" If it were damaged, it would be like losing my best friend. No, it was safe under my bed. I was so relieved I wanted to laugh, but I was still so shaken by the explosion that laughter was impossible.

Someone knocked on our door. When Don opened it, there were Kitty Barret and Phyllis "P.J." Clever, the two women on our show. They had also been knocked out of their beds by the blast. "Come down to the basement," Kitty said. "Everyone else is there. It should be much safer."

There we found about fifty terrified civilians, huddled together, wondering what might happen next.

I had carried my accordion along with me and started playing it very softly. The melodies were familiar and soothing. Kitty and P.J. started to sing, and it wasn't long before everyone was singing or humming along with us. Music transcended language barriers, and at midnight we sang "Auld Lang Syne" as I had never heard it sung before—or have since.

Then Sandy Rozell, a Scotsman who wore kilts and combat boots in his act, brought out his little soprano saxophone and lightened our mood even more. For a little while, we were able to forget that we were in the middle of an inferno. Music provided us with a small island of peace.

Two hours later, we were back in our rooms; the bombing had ended, and the night was so quiet I couldn't sleep. At a little writing table, I began a letter to my fiancée, Berdyne. I asked her not to worry: I was eating

3

regularly, practicing a lot, and missing her. But I didn't mention our close call.

In the morning as Don and I walked to the 3038th Quartermaster Bakery Company for breakfast, we saw people everywhere digging out from under the wreckage. An old Dutch woman, dazed and crying, sat on a pile of rubble—all that was left of the hostel she had owned and managed. It had been destroyed by the very bomb that had knocked us out of bed. And less than a block from our hostel!

Later that morning I visited a badly damaged church. The sun was shining through a gaping hole that had once been a stained-glass window. I knelt at the altar to thank the Lord for sparing my life. I prayed that I would not disappoint Him during whatever time I had left. I gave Him my trust as I had been called upon to do many times before...

Ever since I was a young boy on the farm in South Dakota.

The Roaring (?) Twenties

The twenties on the farms in South Dakota were anything but "roaring." "Groaning" would be a better description. While people elsewhere seemed to be making lots of money, we in the Midwest had a hard time just making ends meet. Even Mother Nature would work against us. Just when crops and prices would begin to look good, we'd be struck by hailstorms or grasshoppers, and our livelihood would be threatened or even wiped out. One storm when I was about seven is still fresh in my mind.

"Looks like this crop will yield a good thirty-five bushels to the acre. We can start harvesting early next week," Pa said one day as he ground a couple heads of wheat in his hand, blew away the chaff, and showed the grain to my brother Arlie and me. We were standing in a forty-acre wheat field west of the house. The grain stood a foot taller than five-year-old Arlie and even a few inches above my head. It was a breezy day, and when I stood on tiptoe, I could see waves on the field much like the waves on water.

"It's been a good year," Pa continued. "Just enough rain, no grasshoppers, and a pretty fair price at the elevator. We'll have a good winter."

Just then I felt a splatter of rain hit my forehead. Pa's expression turned to deep concern as he, too, felt the raindrops. In the western sky an ominous cloud appeared. The wind picked up, creating little twisters in the dust and tiny whirlpools in the field of wheat.

"Better get inside. Looks like we're going to have a little shower," Pa said as he rushed us toward the house.

By the time we reached the front steps, we were drenched by rain. No sooner had we slammed the door behind us than the hailstorm broke in all its fury. In minutes the ground was covered with white hailstones, some of them as large as chicken's eggs.

Almost immediately the brilliant flashes of lightning and simultaneous crashes of thunder signaled that we were in the very center of the storm. But as the time interval between the two lengthened, we knew the storm would soon be past.

Half an hour after I had felt the first raindrops, the storm had ended. The ground was covered with hail, and there were little rivers of water in the front yard. The ground had had its fill of moisture, and the excess was making its way to the slough below the barn. Pa opened the front door very slowly, put on his galoshes, and, with Arlie and me following, walked to the field we had been admiring such a short time before. Those beautiful stalks of wheat had been pounded flat—a whole year's work and planning had been shattered in a few minutes.

"Don't worry," Pa said sorrowfully as he held a stalk in his hand. "We can probably save about ten percent of this. Next year, with God's help and our sweat, will be better."

We put away the mail-order catalogs, and Ma started patching our well-worn clothing. "That's good for a few more miles," Pa said, and Ma sang a little Norwegian song

6

to herself as she sewed. Some of Ma's patches lasted longer than the clothes she mended.

In spite of hardships, farm life had its virtues. It bound the family close and taught us much about honesty, integrity, and respect for good hard work.

Our small "grain farm" consisted of 120 acres. Dad's older brother Olaf owned the farm next to ours. My cousins Martin, Myrtle, and George were all older than I. Besides our pasture, the yearly crops included about 30 acres of wheat, 10 of barley, and several acres each of corn, alfalfa, clover, and flax. To help keep the land fertile we would rotate the crops. Where we grew clover one year, corn would follow the next season, barley, oats or wheat the next, and then back to clover. What one crop took out of the soil the next would put back in. Putting corn in an area would help keep down the weeds. Manure from the barn was put back in the fields for fertilizer. We always planted a few acres of vegetables, especially potatoes and rutabagas—the staples for winter. One year we gambled (and won) on an acre of onions. We also raised cows, horses, pigs, and chickens. Each animal required care, and chores were assigned to each of us children according to our abilities. Today, whenever people ask me how I achieved my technique on the accordion, I answer, "By milking the cows on the farm." The process of milking by hand helped to develop the exceptional strength in the fingers and forearms so necessary for any keyboard.

I was about eight years old when Pa heard of a small Fordson tractor that had been scrapped near his brother Mike's farm in Dell Rapids. After we rented the truck to haul it home, Pa, Arlie, and I turned that piece of scrap into a fine tractor. Then Pa converted our heavier machinery so it could all be pulled by the tractor instead of our horses. Our threshing machine was so much larger than the Fordson that to this day I remember it as a Pekinese pulling a Great Dane!

We also altered the engine to run on "distillate" (a kerosene fuel slightly less refined than diesel). With gasoline at fifteen cents a gallon and distillate less than half that, we'd start the engine on gasoline, run it all day on distillate, and then switch back to gasoline for a few minutes at the end of the day to clean out the valves.

A large family was essential to a farm, because, as the children grew in size and number, more work could be done. I was the oldest in our family, followed by my brother Arlie, my sisters Valborg, Genevieve, Virginia, and Gloria, and finally by my youngest brother, Duane. All of us were born at home and at night. As Ma's time approached, Pa would stay close to the house so he could call the doctor. The doctor would usually arrive in the evening with his little black bag, and we children would be sent to bed. When we awoke the next morning, Mother would be nursing another addition to the family.

We each contracted the usual childhood diseases, and there were times when four or five of us would be down with whooping cough, measles, or flu at once. Through it all, Ma and Pa were always cheerful and encouraging, although there must have been times when they would each wonder, "Why me, Lord?"

Ma often suffered attacks of pleurisy and pneumonia; at those times all of us would grow silent and pray. Many times I would be awakened by the sound of Pa's voice as he talked with the doctor and our minister, Reverend Elmer Berg. But I could tell by the changed tone of their voices when Ma had again passed the crisis and was on the road to recovery.

Illness and injury were constant threats on the farm; fortunately though, death was not so common. I was seven years old the first time it struck close to me.

My seventeen-year-old cousin Martin and I were very close; we even shared similar dreams for the future. Martin's future, however, was cut short; he had tuberculosis.

Since fresh air was then thought to be the only treatment for TB, Martin was moved into a tent in front of his father's house. It was midwinter and bitter cold. I could see Martin's ice-covered tent from our living room window. Pa told me that Martin was dying, but I just couldn't believe him. I was convinced that if I watched over him, he would soon be well.

Then one day two men drove up in a hearse and walked into the tent with Martin's father. They came out a few minutes later carrying a shrouded bundle. I was shocked to realize that it was Martin's body. Like most Norwegian-American children, I had always been taught to keep my emotions under control, so I went on to do my chores and tried to put the loss of Martin out of my mind.

But toward the end of the funeral three days later, as Martin was being carried to the burial ground outside the church, my emotions broke loose. I wept uncontrollably; Pa had to hold me up. While Mother said goodbye to the family, Pa said to me, "Well, we'd better get back home and do the chores. The cows need milking and the chicks will be hungry." He was no psychologist, but he knew that the best cure for grief was hard work.

Hard work was easy to find on the farm, but entertainment was scarce. Our radio ran on storage batteries that Pa would take to town to be recharged when necessary. We listened to weather reports and D. B. Gurney and his farm reports. Sometimes we would hear Lawrence Welk and his Hotsy Totsy Boys, or Happy Bill and the Old Timers on WNAX, Yankton, South Dakota. On Saturday nights, if the weather was just right, we could hear the "National Barn Dance" on WLS all the way from Chicago. I kept a list of the three-dial settings needed for each station.

During summers, we all looked forward to our drives to Pickerel Lake, about fifteen miles to the east of our farm, to visit with relatives and friends, swim, and eat a big lunch. Ma and the other women really outdid themselves at those picnics. They would work all morning fixing potato salad, fried chicken, ham sandwiches, hard-boiled eggs, and, as a special treat, *lefse*. *Lefse* is a sort of Norwegian tortilla, made from potatoes and flavored with butter and, sometimes, sugar. It's a treat that I still look forward to today when Betty, my sister-in-law, bakes it for all of us at Christmastime. I always thought that my mother made the best *lefse* anywhere, but Betty's is a very close second! Betty's husband, Ken Hanson, is also of Norwegian extraction.

The main topic of conversation at those gatherings was the number of flat tires we all had driving over. Many inner tubes had more patches than original rubber, thanks to the rather hazardous condition of the roads.

Many of the roads in South Dakota were old wagon trails; few were graveled and not one was paved. We drove in the ruts made by countless wagon wheels, so speeds higher than forty were foolhardy, if not impossible. We surely never needed to balance the tires!

Once or twice a year we made the all-day trip to Dell Rapids, 165 miles away, to visit Pa's family. About five in the morning, after chores, we would start out, stopping for forenoon lunch on the shore of Lake Kampeska, about sixty miles from home. The huge pools of water left in ancient wheel ruts after recent rains made us happy that the front axle of our Model T was set high enough off the ground to drive almost anywhere.

We kids would time our long ride to Dell Rapids by different landmarks along the way. After Lake Kampeska came Lone Tree, a magnificent cottonwood that had been spared by the road builders 12 miles north of Dell Rapids. We would stop here about sundown to stretch and admire this natural wonder. At the time few trees in South Dakota could boast the size and history of this grand old monarch. We would drive on a straight road to Dell Rapids and then test the mettle of the Model T on the muddy three mile road to Uncle Mike's farm.

As our family grew in number and age, Burma Shave signs were added to our landmarks. The first one I remember was near home and read, "If you don't know whose signs these are, you can't have driven very far—Burma Shave." About halfway we'd come to "Every shaver now can snore, six more minutes than before by using Burma Shave." And then, near Dell Rapids we would read, "Jonah took no brush to mop his face, when Jonah went he needed space—Burma Shave." Then I knew that our trip was soon to be over. Generally this one would be lit by the headlights of our trusty Model T, and all of us youngsters would wake up, get our things together, and be ready to greet Uncle Mike, Grandpa Ole, and Aunt Olga. We would all pitch in to help Uncle Mike finish his chores because we knew the sooner the chores were finished the sooner we would enjoy Aunt Olga's super cooking. I would think of Cousin George doing the chores on our farm and wonder if any of our animals missed us.

We used the Model T during harvest season to take lunch to the threshing crews in the fields. As a field was harvested, a six-to-ten-inch stubble was left behind. That

11

stubble would hide rocks that could really damage a car if it was not built high enough to avoid them.

Pa bought an Essex in 1926, and while the neighbors all thought the car was real pretty, their unanimous opinion was that it would be useless, because there was not enough clearance under the front axle. Sure enough, the first time we tried to drive across a field, we hit a rock and knocked a hole in the oil pan.

Now, you may be wondering how we got the car to the repair shop to fix the oil pan. No problem. Pa just jacked the car up right there, got out his tools, and removed the oil pan. His brother, Olaf, drove him to Roslyn, where they got it welded. Back again in the field, they put the oil pan back on the car, filled the engine with oil, and were ready to go. All in less than two hours!

Driving was always an adventure; even when we had to get out and push, it was a labor of love. In warm weather we'd remove the side curtains for some natural air conditioning, but when it started to rain, we could replace them in short order and be almost watertight. When I grew tall enough, my job was to operate the hand-powered windshield wipers.

It's unfortunate that today's young people will never feel the thrill of starting an engine with a handcrank. Of course we always had to be careful; if the handle wasn't held just right, a backfire could result in a broken thumb! When I was very small, Pa taught me to work the throttle levers while he cranked. I would listen for the first sign of life from the motor and then quickly set the levers to the predetermined positions. But there were times when the car would prove balky and not start—usually when we were already late for church. Then we would sit quietly, trying not to get dirty, while Pa coaxed the engine into starting. The only way I could tell when he was becoming

12

upset was when he would shake his head and mutter, "Shucks!" or "Shavings!" That was the closest I ever heard him come to swearing.

Many of our friends and neighbors had trouble getting used to the change from horse-drawn buggies to motorized cars. But no one had more trouble than Oskar, a friend of my grandfather, Tom Lensegrav, on Ma's side of the family. Oskar was positively the worst driver in the entire county. He always thought a car could be handled just like a horse, and *that* got him into a lot of trouble. Oskar could start his beat-up old Model T just fine, but when it came time to stop, he would become excited and forget to use the brakes. As a result, we were often treated to the sight of Oskar careening down the road, waving his hands in the air, yelling, "Whoa! Consarn it! Whoa!!"

One afternoon Grandpa was out for a drive in his own brand-new Model T when he saw Oskar driving toward him on the same road. Well, he didn't want Oskar to run into his new car, so Grandpa drove off the road into the cornfield to avoid him. When Oskar saw Grandpa swerve off the road, he said to himself, "There must be some awful big hole in the road for Tom to go way around it like that! I'd better do the same." So Oskar followed Grandpa off the road and hit his new Model T head-on thirty-five feet out in the cornfield!

We lived about four miles southwest of Roslyn, a town of nearly 140 people. Webster, the county seat, was ten miles to the south. Saturday night was *the* night in Roslyn; how I loved to lean on the fender of the Ford and watch the people go by! Baukol's Store was right in the center of the town; the First National Bank and Gottschalk's Store were across the street. The town band shell, where we could watch silent cartoons every Saturday night during summer, was across the street from Gottschalk's. Our favorite cartoons were Felix the Cat and Popeye (they were also the *only* cartoons!).

Mother did all our shopping in Roslyn, and with four daughters in the family, she was always looking for bargains in dress goods. The market crash of 1929 affected those of us who didn't own stocks too, and we saved wherever we could. All my sisters' dresses and most of the clothing for the boys in the family were made on Ma's peddle-power Singer sewing machine, and that first machine was still giving good service when she passed away in 1978 at the age of eighty-two.

About this time, too, I remember my Uncle Adolph Thornegs was selling Maytag washing machines—run by little gasoline motors. Where washing used to be an all-day affair with hand wringers and many tubs for washing and blueing, the job became much easier. In the summer we'd do the laundry outside and in the winter in the basement. The fumes from that little gasoline motor used to be rather overpowering until Pa rigged up a long hose to the basement window. That Maytag, too, is still giving service washing clothes for great-grandchildren north of Sioux Falls, the only difference being that Pa replaced the engine with an electric motor when that power became available in Webster.

I had my first haircut at Elmer Vevang's barbershop when I was three years old. My hair fell almost to my waist (I'll bet some of you thought long hair didn't come into style until the sixties!). I stopped in to see Elmer in May 1980; he still had the board he used to place across the arms of his barber chair for his youngest customers.

I still think the ice cream cones I could buy for just five cents at Starkey's Drug Store were the best treats I've ever had. Starkey's is also where I first discovered pulp magazines; cowboys, Indians, and airplanes made the greatest impression on me. The adventures of steely-eyed cowboy heroes of the Old West and those of Captain Eddie Rickenbacker in the air wars of World War I no doubt gave me more pleasure and thrills than most television shows give kids today.

The Roslyn Consolidated School was a two-story building not far from the community hall. Grades one through twelve were combined in the one school, and children were "bused" in from all the surrounding farms. For a few years, Pa was our bus driver. In good weather he used the Model T, but during the winter he would use the horse-drawn sleigh. We'd all be bundled up in heavy blankets and have hot soapstones, warmed on the kitchen stove, under our feet. Pa always believed that if your feet were kept warm, your whole body would be warm.

Light snow was falling one winter afternoon when Pa picked us up in the sleigh. Suddenly the wind started to howl, and before we were halfway home, the light snow had turned into a real blizzard. The temperature dropped to about thirty-five below zero, and the wind cut into us like an icy knife. Pa just let the reins fall slack, and our trusty horses, with long icicles hanging from their mouths, brought us safely home.

In the basement of the school were the gym, shop classes, restrooms, and the furnace. During the winter we boys would spend our fifteen-minute recess periods chinning ourselves on a convenient two-by-four in our rest room. In good weather we played softball. I played left field. I enjoyed sports, but it seems as if I was always getting hurt, spraining something, or getting into silly scrapes that would keep me out of the big games. Running was the easiest exercise to do alone on the farm, so after every illness, sprain or accident I would be back running—to the

15

mailbox a quarter-mile away, to the fields, rounding up the cows for milking—I loved running then and I love it now. As I look back on it, it almost seems that some Divine Providence used these accidents to steer me away from sports and toward music.

Pa had taught me to read and print before I started school, so by the time I was in the second grade, I was reading everything I could get my hands on. One of my favorites, *Decorah Posten*, the Norwegian-language newspaper printed in Decorah, Iowa, was a must in every Norwegian-American household. Its weekly story section, *Ved Arnen* ("with Arnen"), always had Ma and Pa laughing until their sides hurt and they had tears in their eyes.

Our attic was a storehouse of buried treasure. One day when rain kept us out of the fields, I was searching through there and found a half-dozen books that became windows through which I could see a whole world away from the farm. I still remember them: *Know Thyself* by Ralph Waldo Emerson, stories about Horatio Alger and Jack Armstrong, collections by Edgar Rice Burroughs and Zane Grey, a handful of *Popular Mechanics* and *Popular Science* magazines, and, best of all, a geography book. I would stare at those maps and try to imagine myself walking along the Nile or sailing the fjords of Norway. The dreams these books inspired must surely have been conspiring with another love I had to get me off the farm.

Airplanes also interested me; I've been in love with flying ever since I can remember. On one of my earliest trips to the Day County Fair in Webster, I was fascinated by a couple of young men who were selling rides in an open-cockpit airplane. Pa and I soon forgot about the rest of the fair as we watched one after another of our friends

16

fly up in the air and around the fairgrounds. I knew we couldn't afford the two dollars they charged for a ride, so I didn't embarrass Pa by asking to go (although I would have given almost anything for a ride!). We stood by the fence all morning until finally one of the flyers, a tall, thin man, walked over and spoke to us.

"It's safer than riding in your own car," he said. And then, because he seemed to sense our intense interest and lack of funds, he stayed nearby most of the afternoon talking and explaining the operation of the airplane. Finally, as his partner was winding up for the day, he said, "I'm Charles Lindbergh from Minnesota. Someday you'll all be flying!"

As Mr. Lindbergh walked away, Pa said, "He's a Swede, you know." Well! That really sold me, because I knew that *Swedes* were second only to *Norwegians* in the accomplishment of daring deeds.

It was only the following May that the whole world would come to know and love The Lone Eagle as the first person to fly solo across the Atlantic Ocean.

Winter evenings at home were long, but we were never bored. Ma would knit, sew, or crochet; Pa usually spent the evenings reading; and my brothers and sisters did their homework. When chores and schoolwork were finished, I worked on model ships from plans in *Popular Science* magazine. The kerosene lamps cast a dim light over the room where we all gathered near the warmth of our "central heating," a big stove where we burned wood, cow chips, or coal. We were also warmed by the intense feeling of family love, generated, of course, by Pa and Mother. Such love softened the hardships of life on the farm and made us grateful for daily blessings and for each other.

17

Winter evenings were also an opportunity to study for our confirmation in the Lutheran faith, a practice called "reading for the minister." It was a year-long process that also required getting to the church in Roslyn every Saturday morning for catechism classes. As part of our statement of faith, we were expected to memorize the entire catechism. My interest in running as a sport must have developed at this time, because I would run the four miles to Roslyn while reciting the lessons I had memorized. During the winter I would recite while skiing to class on my handmade wooden skis. When I first started to ski, my "boards" were about six feet long, but numerous accidents made them shorter and shorter until, the last I can remember using them, they came only up to my waist.

My parents' most prized possession was a large Norwegian Bible. It was, and still is, the most beautiful book I have ever seen—bound in leather with pictures all through it and with very beautifully styled printing. I learned a good part of my Norwegian from that Good Book, since Ma and Pa read to us from it every evening.

Itinerant ministers called on us from time to time, and of course they were invited to spend the night. During these visits, I would listen to Pa and the minister arguing about the meaning of various verses in the Good Book. Some of their discussions would go on through the night. Ma usually just listened and brought them countless cups of coffee to keep the talk going. I don't remember anyone actually winning these arguments, but Pa sure could hold his own. My concept of Christianity evolved from these conversations. I've always believed the Golden Rule— "Do unto others as you would have them do unto you." Respect for the rights of all people has been the very basis of my faith. Pa always took issue with the idea that the Lord was some terrible avenging god just waiting to start

18

passing out punishments. Instead, he showed us a God of warmth and unending love, a God always ready with an understanding spirit and a helping hand.

Christmas has always been a very special time for me, a time to reaffirm my faith in God and to indulge my affection for my family. And when I was a child, it was also a very special day.

"Look! Santa got his whiskers caught in the window!" I heard my three-year-old sister, Virginia, call excitedly one year. Sure enough, there were a few strands of white hair caught on the windowsill. Since we had no fireplace, we weren't surprised that Santa Claus had to come through a window. (Of course Arlie [9] and I didn't mention that we had seen Pa cutting some hairs from the tail of one of our horses the day before!)

We all knew that Santa brought toys to good children (and we had been *very* good, especially as Christmas grew near). From the window we dashed to the living room and found that, yes, Santa had exchanged the little plate of cookies we had left for him for stockings filled with oranges, apples, nuts, and Cracker Jacks. Best of all, there were presents under the tree we had decorated with candles, popcorn strings, and other homemade ornaments. For Ma and Pa the gifts were mostly drawings we had made at school.

"Can we open our gifts now?" My sister Valborg (7) grabbed Pa's hand and led him to the tree. Pa read the names on the presents and passed them out. Each of the girls received a doll with a little box of doll clothes. They began dressing and playing with them as Arlie and I opened our gifts. Nine-year-old Arlie loved to build things, so Pa bought him a set of Tinker Toys; within minutes he had started to build a windmill. Ma knew how much I loved games, so she chose dominoes for me.

"We better have some breakfast; there's a long day ahead of us," Pa said. He was referring to our annual holiday visit to Ma's family—the Lensegravs, an hour and a half by sleigh.

Mother had gotten up early to prepare our favorite foods for Christmas breakfast: fried eggs, coffee with heavy cream and sugar, mush, toast, and fried *klub*. (*Klub* is a dumpling made with potatoes and whole wheat flour, then sliced and fried.) We all agreed we were eating like kings!

Then we rushed to dress warmly for the sleigh ride. We were really excited; the Lensegravs would have lots of cookies, cheese, sausage, and *lefse*. And Grandpa Lensegrav sure did love his *lefse*; for him no holiday was complete without *lefse* piled high with sugar and fresh butter. When I would comment, too, on how good it was, Grandma would beam and say, "Now here's a *real* Norwegian!" That supreme compliment would warm me for weeks!

Grandpa's little black dog would announce our arrival; then Grandpa and Uncle Halvor would lead the horses off to the barn to be fed and sheltered until we left. Into the house we would rush to be greeted by uncles, cousins, and aunts galore (Ma had one brother and nine sisters). Games, laughter, gifts, and excited conversation filled the afternoon until we were called to dinner, a feast of *lefse, lutefisk,* head cheese, turkey, and pumpkin pie. Then a final round of coffee and conversation before, exhausted, we were packed into our sleigh to sleep during the trip home.

Pa used to tease Grandpa Lensegrav about having to keep a baseball bat to control the boys visiting the "beautiful Lensegrav sisters." I was into my teens before I fully understood what he was talking about; all my aunts *were* really beautiful! But as I write this, Emma Nerland, Minnie Thorness, Anna Anderson, and Thilde Floren (my mother) have all passed on. Halvor Lensegrav died many years ago in South Dakota. Josie Hagen lives in Livermore, California, near most of her children. Inga Lyle, Agnes Alwin, and Lillian Ahlers settled in Seattle, Washington. Two sisters still live in South Dakota: Esther Farness in Webster and Laura Smith in Kidder. Laura's husband Melvin is my only remaining uncle.

I have such pleasant memories of the entire Lensegrav family faithfully attending our little Lutheran church each Sunday. And I can imagine how proud Grandpa must have been of his ten beautiful children, because I know how proud I've always felt whenever I've had a chance to take my six beautiful young women (my wife Berdyne and our daughters Randee, Kristie, Robin, Holly, and Heidi) out with me!

Problems and Opportunities

Sometimes when things seem to be going just right, something will suddenly intrude to break the spell. Then it becomes important to get on top of the situation before one's dreams are permanently smothered. Understanding and overcoming such situations can propel one to even greater heights of accomplishment than previously thought of. And sometimes the misfortune turns out not to be a misfortune at all, but an act of Providence.

That is what happened to me.

In spite of the personal fulfillment that came from the joys and problems of living on the farm, and in spite of the dedication and love my parents and I felt for each other, I decided at an early age that farm life would never satisfy me.

Something kept tugging to pull me away. I could not get it out of my system. It was uppermost in my dreams. It was music. I was infatuated with music.

Pa purchased an organ for Mother soon after they were married. Even before I started school, it fascinated me, and I spent hours trying to play it. Pa finally made a chord chart, and it wasn't long before I could accompany him when he played the fiddle.

I was very proud of what I could do on the organ, but by the time I was seven, I knew it wasn't for me. My interest shifted to a semitone accordion the very moment a local farmer named Johnny Bjugan took it out of its case and played it for me. Within moments I knew that an accordion had to be part of my dreams. I finally persuaded Pa to buy me an accordion. We studied all the pictures in Montgomery Ward and Sears Roebuck and finally settled on one from Sears. It cost $9.95—a fortune then! But it was so pretty in the catalog—ten buttons on the right hand and two bass buttons on the left. I could hardly wait until we had saved enough money to order it.

In just two days it arrived. I'm sure I set an Olympic record running the quarter mile from the mailbox to our home.

I had expected instant mastery, but after about three hours of trying to play, I realized it didn't fit me; it was just too small.

When Ma sent me to the fields with Pa's lunch that afternoon, I carried the accordion along. "Pa," I said as he sat eating a peanut butter sandwich and drinking coffee, "This accordion just isn't big enough for me. I need one like Johnny's."

He didn't answer at once, but finished his lunch, then rolled a cigarette from a can of Prince Albert tobacco. Finally, "Yes, I think you need a bigger one, too. Tomorrow we'll box that one up and order another."

My feet never touched the ground all the way home. The box was ready to be mailed when Pa reached the house that night. Three days later my new, big accordion arrived—a Hohner semitone with twenty-one buttons on the

24

right hand and eight bass buttons on the left. Now I could play in two major keys. I added shoulder straps and used adhesive tape to cover holes whenever they developed in the bellows.

I still have that old "button box" today. Now and then I take it out and play it again. Memories flood over me as I play some of the simple old tunes from so long ago.

Pa seemed to recognize some God-given gift in me. He figured anything he did that thwarted the full exercise of that gift would be going against the Lord's plan for my life. And so he helped me along the way with money or simply, and more importantly, by sitting back and listening to my dreams as we talked. Communication was good between us, and though Pa wasn't a man given to tremendous outward displays of affection, he showed his belief in me in ways I never failed to understand.

I learned all the songs Pa played on the fiddle: lots of Norwegian waltzes, schottisches, and polkas. I progressed pretty well, but still had not learned to read music.

Late one evening, a Harms Piano Company truck stopped at our farm. The driver introduced himself to Pa and explained that the piano on the truck had been meant for a family who had moved without telling the store manager. Now it had to be taken all the way back to Harms' store, fifty miles away in Aberdeen. Pa and the driver came to an agreement. I found out later that Pa had paid fifty dollars for it. It is still in the family.

At school, Miss Dorothy Swenson, my third and fourth grade teacher, started me on the rudiments of music, but I didn't care especially for the lessons. Whenever I made a mistake, she would hit my knuckles with a ruler. But to this day I thank her for that drive to perfection she encouraged in me.

Early in my freshman year, I had additional instruction from a very fine pianist, Walter Pfitzner, from nearby Aberdeen. He gave weekly piano lessons at the school, and I paid for mine with eggs from our chickens. I progressed rapidly; in fact my tenth lesson was Rachmaninoff's "Prelude in C-sharp minor." But by then it was December, and the weather became very cold. After the first freeze, the hens quit laying, and that was the end of my piano lessons. But by that time I had learned enough about reading music to continue on my own.

I became my own most severe critic. As I learned to play more and more songs on the accordion, Pa would let me take it to town on Saturday nights to play for the customers in the grocery store. Sometimes I would get fifty cents for "entertaining." I was eight years old when I played my first really professional job. It was at the Day County Fair, and I earned ten dollars for three days' work.

May 17 is called *Syttende Mai*—it is Norwegian Independence Day, and no Norwegian would be caught dead without celebrating. Well, I remember the celebration one year in Roslyn when I was nine or ten. A band was playing at the community hall on the east side of Main Street. I sat in the front row of the audience all evening, my eyes glued to the conductor playing an accordion, forgetting all the carnival rides, games, and food outside. I imagined myself up there on the stage entertaining all those people. I became more determined than ever before to make accordion playing my life's work. But would I ever be able to play as well as that conductor was playing? I heard somebody say he and his band were becoming famous. It was Lawrence Welk.

Summer vacation at Roslyn High School was only six weeks away, and the spring weather was better than ever. All my freshman year we had played softball nearly every

26

day during recess and lunch hours. I loved playing left field because I enjoyed running to catch the balls those farm boys slugged out. No matter how hard they batted toward left field, when the ball came down, I was there to grab it...even when I sometimes had to run across the street and jump a ditch!

We played hard because time was limited. The fields were drying out, and soon we would be needed to start the spring planting. Winter had blessed us with lots of snow, and the rich, black soil was ready for the seeds that we hoped would produce a bumper crop.

My throat felt very sore after one very active Friday game. "Just dry," I thought, and I drank a lot of water that evening. But I shivered as I prepared for bed, and soon I was unable to control the chills. By morning I had a high fever and a strep throat. But it was Saturday, and I thought I could sleep it off over the weekend; there was still plenty of time to get well and do my part of the spring planting. Then Sunday and Monday passed. No improvement. In fact, my throat was much worse, and I had lost my appetite. It was even difficult to swallow water.

After a week in bed I was still weak, but I felt a little better and decided to return to school. I managed to concentrate on the lessons I had missed, and my teachers arranged a schedule of make-up tests. But days later my strength had not returned. The chills hit me again, this time accompanied by sharp pains in both wrists. I recognized these symptoms. I had had rheumatic fever twice before, once before I started school, and again when I was in the fourth grade. Yes, I knew it was rheumatic fever this time, too.

By the following morning every joint in my body hurt, and even the slightest movement of the bed would cause me to cry out in pain.

Over the next two weeks I became weaker and weaker. I had no appetite at all, and I could feel pain settling around my heart. Breathing became a chore. With every deep breath, sharp pains would shoot through my chest.

"We've got a very sick boy here, Doctor. Can you come out right away?... Thanks, Doc. We'll see you this afternoon." I heard Pa on the phone, his voice heavy with concern as he spoke to the doctor in Webster.

Dr. William Duncan listened to my heart for a long time without speaking. When he finally looked up, I could see dread in his eyes. Haltingly and in a low voice, he spoke to Pa and Mother. "The fever has gone to his heart, and the lining is infected. There is a lot of pus that should be drained around the heart muscle, but he's too weak to stand the strain. I'll stay here tonight. If he can make it through the night, he may have a chance of pulling through. We can only wait."

As the evening wore on, the house became quiet, and I could hear Pa and Mother talking with the doctor in the next room from time to time. It was very late before Pa went out to do the chores, but no matter what, the livestock had to be cared for. "I should be helping him," I thought feverishly. He had to milk the cows, feed the horses, pigs, and chickens, and gather the eggs and get the animals all settled for the night. Alone, it would take him hours. I seemed to be more upset about not doing my share the past few weeks than I was about being so sick!

It was a long, long night. Each time I fell asleep, the same dream recurred. I was being chased by a huge, crazed, and rabid dog. I knew if it bit me, a terrible death awaited me. It chased me through a thick, dark forest, branches clawing at me, slowing me down. I fell, and the dog was right on top of me. I screamed out loud. Then suddenly Pa

28

and Ma were standing by my bed with Dr. Duncan saying, "It's all right. Everything is going to be fine. You'll be feeling better soon." Arlie, Valborg, and Genevieve stood together at the door, their faces reflecting the fear they felt for me.

"Pa! Ma!" I said. "I'm scared! I feel like I'm going through a big dark forest, and I'm lost. I can't get out. I'm afraid to be alone. Stay with me for just a few minutes. Won't you stay with me?" Both nodded, and I settled back, hoping to get some sleep without the intrusion of that terrible nightmare.

I had noticed that the big family Bible was on the dresser; it hadn't been there before. That's when I knew that Pa would stay right with me, because he had carried the Bible into my room to help give me strength.

Finally sleep did come over me, but as I drifted off, I felt myself rising up out of my body. I looked down and saw it lying on the bed far below. I saw the worried looks on the faces of my family. But as I drifted upward, I began to feel free and happy. I wondered if this were death, and if it were, why I had been so frightened by it. Then the same dream returned: the dog, more vicious than ever, was coming closer all the time. Fear made my heart pound, and sweat poured from me as I made a last desperate effort to escape. The forest suddenly ended at a steep cliff, and I felt myself falling down while the dog, at the top, howled in frustration.

My fall was gradually slowed, and a great peace came over me. I was floating on a cloud. A full moon drove away the darkness. I heard myself saying, "I have died. I am with God. What a wonderful place heaven is." God's presence was everywhere, and I could feel good health and happiness all around me. Best of all, I could hear music in the distance!

29

I leaned back on my cloud pillow and felt strength and life flowing back into me. Then all movement stopped, and I came to rest back on my own bed. Gradually I began to recognize Ma, Pa, Arlie, and my sisters, who had clustered around me. Dr. Duncan leaned over and listened to my heart. "The fever has broken," he said. "He's going to make it!" I was drenched with sweat, but I felt better than I had in weeks, and I was *hungry* at last.

"Could I have some bacon and eggs for breakfast?" I asked. Ma, with a prayer of thanksgiving on her face, smiled happily and hurried off toward the kitchen.

"It's a miracle," Dr. Duncan said to Pa. "Last night I wouldn't have given a plugged nickel for his chances. A Greater Power just pulled him through. I believe God is looking out for him." Pa walked to the dresser and picked up the Bible. He was reading softly when Ma returned with my first meal in over two weeks. "The Lord is my shepherd; I shall not want," he read out loud. Dr. Duncan and Ma echoed, "Amen!"

In spite of my being down to less than one hundred pounds, it wasn't long before I was feeling much like my old self again.

In May 1980 I appeared as guest of the Roslyn chapter of the Future Farmers of America. Many members of my original school were there including Dorothy Swenson (now Mrs. Helmer Foss) and Lloyd Haisch, my FFA teacher. My Aunt Laura and Uncle Melvin Smith were also there. Recalling the time of my rheumatic fever attack when I was a Roslyn freshman, Mr. Haisch said the FFA class visited me one day because he'd heard I was dying and thought they could give me some comfort. I remember their visit as in a dream, and if my memory serves me correctly, it was later that same day that Dr. Duncan was called to come out.

I remember, too, Reverend Berg's coming out and reading the Bible and praying a long time at my bedside. Just before he entered my room, I heard Dad tell him, "...and be careful what you say; he's awful sick, but he's not going to die."

Rheumatic fever taught me a lot. I learned that just when it seems all doors to opportunity have closed, more will open. This had happened to Glenn Cunningham, the runner from Kansas who held the world's record for the mile for so many years; after a crippling disease he overcame adversity and became the toast of the sports world.

Now rheumatic fever had closed the door to any lingering thoughts I may have had of becoming active in sports, but the damage to my heart opened the door I needed to walk through if nothing were to interfere with music as my life's work.

While recuperating, I spent hours practicing my accordion and polishing my ability to read and write music. My illness gave me a desire to live my life to the fullest; to me that meant total devotion to music.

Today I enjoy music more than ever, and I wish I could continue working for a hundred years! As my good friend Tom Purdum of the New Braunfels Chamber of Commerce in Texas says, "There are no problems, only opportunities!"

Music and
Politics

Although I had decided that music was to be my career, it was a combination of poor crops and politics that actually started me on that career.

During the early thirties, Uncle Olaf Floren became involved in local politics as Treasurer of Day County. At the end of his second term, he decided to run for Registrar of Deeds. Since we were having a spell of very bad luck on the farm, Pa wanted to try for the office his brother was leaving. At first Uncle Olaf objected, thinking that the people of Day County would frown on two brothers holding public office at the same time. But finally he gave Pa his blessing, realizing probably that Pa would run regardless, and Uncle Olaf also didn't want to sow any seeds of discord between the two families.

After chores one evening, Pa and I sat together watching the sunset. The animals had all been fed and bedded down for the night, and the combination of contented animals and gentle weather combined to put him in a thoughtful mood. It seemed a good time for me to bring up a problem.

"You know, Pa, I need a professional accordion if I am going to make a living out of music. Do you think we could afford one if you are elected? Could we think about it?"

True to his custom when a problem was brought up, Pa didn't say anything for a long time. And he rolled a cigarette as he watched the sunset. His hesitation was a good sign; the longer he took to answer a question, the more sure I was that he would say yes.

And sure enough. "Yes, I think it is time for you to have a professional accordion. But you know, even if I do win the election, we still won't be rolling in money. The job pays only $141 a month, and we have nine people to care for. I know you have a real talent for music and will work hard to accomplish whatever you set out to do. Yes, we'll try to get you a bigger accordion if I am elected."

Pa had his work cut out for him now; besides the work on the farm, he also had to attend political rallies and meetings all over Day County. The first few campaign speeches were not easy for him; his hands shook so much he couldn't roll his cigarettes without spilling most of the tobacco. Eventually he got used to making speeches and actually enjoyed the campaign as he talked, joked, and won the crowds.

Pa took me and my little accordion along to many of the rallies, where I discovered that entertaining and politics have much in common. I discovered that I was ahead if I played what the people wanted to hear, just as Pa benefited from gearing his speeches to the interests of his audiences. I would play polkas and mazurkas if the crowd was mostly Polish; for Norwegians and Swedes I chose waltzes and schottisches. Years later, while I was working with the USO shows in Europe, my friend and comedian Hank Ladd had a favorite saying that summed it up perfectly: "When in Rome, shoot Roman candles!" My boss,

Lawrence Welk, has used the same principle with great success for years—play what the people want to hear, and they will always listen.

At last, election day! Pa and Ma voted early in a little country school near our farm, then went home to do the chores. We had all we could do to wait for the votes to be counted. The long day dragged on. No news from our radio; it was dead! And our phone had also picked *this day* of all days to go on the fritz! Next morning the radio and phone were both still dead!

By seven o'clock, after Pa had finished the chores, he could stand the suspense no longer. I was sent running next door to Uncle Olaf's to find out the results of the election.

I raced to the back door and knocked. Cousin George let me in but motioned for me to be quiet while his father was on the phone. So I listened to Uncle Olaf asking about all the candidates until finally he asked, "And how about county treasurer? . . . Yes, I see; that's very interesting. . . . Thanks a lot. Goodbye."

Uncle Olaf turned away from the phone and pretended to notice me for the first time. "Oh! Good morning, Myron. How about some breakfast? Maybe a cinnamon roll or some cream of wheat?"

He poured himself another cup of coffee as I struggled to control my urge to shout out my question. "Well," I said, "a cinnamon roll would taste pretty good, I guess." (My aunt's rolls were always something special!)

As Uncle Olaf handed me a roll and a cup of coffee, he said to George, "I won the race for registrar of deeds. Guess we had better let Ole know how his race went."

"Myron, when you finish your roll, go tell your Pa that he won the office of treasurer."

Pa won!

I set the roll and coffee down on the counter very carefully and walked as calmly as I could to the door. "Thanks for the news, Uncle," I said quietly. "I'll go tell Pa now."

No sooner had I closed the front door than I ran from the house as fast as I could, taking a shortcut across the pasture where Uncle Olaf's big bull usually stood waiting for a chance to chase me. This time he saw me coming, but his bellow of rage was cut to a startled snort as I sped like a bullet. Early Superman!

I burst through the front door shouting, "Pa! You won! You won!"

Ma was pouring coffee, and Pa was leaning on the kitchen stove having no luck at all rolling a cigarette. "I kind of figured you might have good news when I saw you leave that ornery old bull in the dust just now," he said.

I had never doubted that Pa would be elected, and I had reminded him over and over about our talk that evening at sunset. He would always answer with a smile, "Let's just wait and see." However, I was so confident that I had written to the Hagstrom Company in Sweden for information on their accordions. But due to the spreading war in Europe, no accordions were being made for export.

By early December my folks had moved to Webster, where Pa would take up his post on the second day of January. They rented a house for seventeen dollars a month; with nine people in the family, that was a lot of money for rent. But the school was across the street and the courthouse only a couple blocks away; so they figured we would save money on gasoline by walking to and from work and school. (Gasoline was selling for the outrageously high price of eighteen cents a gallon!)

36

I wanted to finish the first semester of my junior year in Roslyn High School, so I rented a room in a boarding house near the school. I borrowed a piano accordion from a distant relative, Bernard Farmen, and it didn't take me long to decide that a piano accordion was the instrument I needed. But the cost was the drawback—$400! How could I expect Pa to finance something that costly? I decided to wait as long as possible before bringing the subject up again.

During Christmas vacation Roslyn was snowed in. All the roads were closed, and even the daily train could not run. Soon the stores were out of fresh foods and most canned goods. Our only source of milk and eggs was the local farmers who could hitch a team to a sleigh and come to town; that was not often either because the snow was piling deeper every day, and new blizzards closed us in tighter. Travel was dangerous, if not impossible.

Finally I could wait no longer. I was very homesick for my sisters and brothers, and I needed to talk to Pa about my accordion.

The weather was fairly clear one morning, and since the train was not running, I decided to walk the twelve miles to Webster. That walk took more than four hours, and I made it just in time for lunch.

"What are *you* doing here?" they all asked at once. "We thought you'd have to stay in Roslyn with weather so bad."

"Well, I missed all of you, and I wanted to talk to Pa," I answered. "Besides, a little walk seemed like a good idea."

I wandered around Webster for the next few days, trying to see as much as possible before heading back to school. I noticed Cook's Music Store on the south edge of town. The owner and operator was Wesley Cook, the son of a prominent doctor. Pa and I went to see him, and after looking at all the brochures on several accordions, we decided on a Soprani—white mother of pearl with forty-one piano keys and 120 bass buttons, eight switches in the right hand and two in the bass. Just what I needed.

But $385!

"That's much more than I can afford," Pa said. "You know the office of county treasurer doesn't pay very much, and I've got almost more than I can handle now."

Wesley could sense my intense desire for that particular accordion, and he said to Pa, "Why don't you come back in a few days and we'll talk it over; maybe we can arrive at a price that would be fair to both of us."

A day or two later, Pa and Wesley agreed on a price, and the accordion was ordered.

Although I had to return to Roslyn to finish my first semester, I joined my family in Webster for my second semester.

A week or two after the second semester started, I was home for lunch when Ma said, "Oh, Myron, Wesley Cook called to tell you your accordion has arrived."

That afternoon was the only time in my life that I ever skipped school.

Ma's words were barely out of her mouth when I shot through the door to Cook's Music Store. Once there I found a sign on the door: "Out to lunch—Back at Two." It was only twelve-thirty! I wondered if I would live to see two o'clock. I pressed my face to the window and looked in. Sure enough; there on the counter was my accordion. The case was open, and the instrument looked as though it was waiting for me.

Wesley finally returned—at two o'clock sharp. "May I help you?" he asked as if he had never seen me before.

"Well, yes," I answered in what I hoped was the same

casual manner. "I'd like to see an accordion. Do you have any for sale?"

"May have. Just got one in this morning as a matter of fact. Would you like to see it?"

"Yes, I would," I answered, "if you have time to show it to me."

"Well, come in and we'll see what we can do." I could tell that Wesley was getting a kick out of my barely restrained excitement. I never knew he had so many door keys, but finally he got the door open, and we walked inside.

I went right to the accordion, took it off the counter, and started to adjust the straps. I had the instrument already half on my shoulders when Wesley said, "Would you like to try it on?"

Would I?

I quickly adjusted the accordion to fit just right, opened the bellows, and began testing each key. "This is what I have been born to do," I thought as I felt the keys and heard the music. Even though Pa and Wesley hadn't ironed out all the details of the sale, he suggested I take the accordion home and start working with it. I didn't wait for him to change his mind! That thirty-five-pound accordion felt as light as a feather all ten blocks of the way home.

I went to work in earnest on the accordion. I bought all the music I could afford, listened to accordionists on the radio, and practiced constantly. Some of those accordionists I listened to so long ago have become my good friends today; one of them, Lawrence Welk, even became my boss.

But I loved and studied all types of music and spent all my free time listening and learning. Fray and Braggiotti, Mike Dosch, Lulu Belle and Scotty, and Sam and the City Fellers were among my favorites. I never missed a chance to hear the Metropolitan Opera auditions from New York City either.

Aunt Julia Floren, a chiropractor, was also an amateur pianist and artist. She gave me all of her old *Étude* magazines, which I literally devoured from beginning to end. Each issue had a song to be learned, and I would play it first on the piano, then transcribe it for the accordion, and then learn to play it. Practice was never a chore. It was pure fun. I set goals to learn a number of new songs every day; that desire to learn new things is still with me today.

I also learned a lot from the comedians, actors, and newscasters on the radio. Jack Benny and Fred Allen were my favorites; I listened for the style and sense of timing that made them each unique. Today more than ever I can appreciate the hours of rehearsal and hard work that are required if one is to give a top performance.

I hope I never stop learning!

Augustana College
and KSOO

In September of 1938 I enrolled as a freshman at Augustana College in Sioux Falls. The tuition was high, so when I found that my intended major in music would require the rental of a piano at an additional twenty-five dollars a semester, I decided to take a major in English and a minor in music instead. To augment what I learned in music classes, I sang in Carl Youngdahl's chapel choir and played bass viol in the college orchestra. When I mentioned to Richard Guderyahn, its director, that I played the accordian, he informed me rather coolly that no orchestra music was ever written for the accordion. "Well," I thought to myself, "maybe not *now*, but just wait!"

One evening shortly after classes had started, I was practicing the accordion when there was a knock on my door. I recognized the fellow standing there as Ray Plowman of Watertown, one of the more popular football players on campus.

"Hi, Myron," he said very cordially. "We were wondering if you would come downstairs and play for everyone in the reception hall."

Of course I was delighted for an opportunity to get to know a few people (and also to forget some of my homesickness). So I went down and played an impromptu concert for a couple of hours. I enjoyed it, and my audience seemed to enjoy it, too.

Actually it was only a few months ago when I learned that the performance was really part of my initiation, or hazing, into college life—and here all this time I had thought that my musical talent was *finally* being fully appreciated!

My roommate, Howard Hillman, was from Lennox. Since we were both freshmen and from similar farm backgrounds, we became great friends and helped each other endure those first lonely days away from home.

Once settled in at college, I paid a visit to Radio Station KSOO, looking for some work. Mr. Joe Henkin, the station owner, was very cordial, but he said they used only records. The only live programs were the newscasts. He took me on a tour of the station; I met his son, Mort, and many of the other employees, including Don Harvey, the resident disc jockey. But as Mr. Henkin ushered me out the door, he uttered the famous show-biz turndown, "Don't call us; we'll call you." Of course, being fresh off the farm, I didn't know that when translated, what he had said meant, "We have no intention of hiring you!"

A couple of weeks later I ran into Mr. Henkin at a Kiwanis meeting, where I was entertaining. I told him I'd been so busy that even though he might have called, I had not received the message. He acted sort of surprised and then said, "Why don't you come down tomorrow morning? We may have something for you to do."

I was waiting with my accordion when they opened the doors at KSOO the next day.

"We have a harness company that would like a live

music show early in the morning. It doesn't pay much—
only ten dollars a week, and it will mean five mornings a
week at seven o'clock."

"I'll take it," I said. I didn't tell him that I would have
been willing to do the show for free!

"There's only one problem," Mr. Henkin continued.
"We'll have to change your name to something easy like
John Smith—a name everyone can remember."

I answered that I liked my own name and would just
as soon keep it, since I didn't want to hurt my parents'
feelings. Then Don Harvey spoke up: "Why don't we keep
the name and invent a title like Song Stylist or the Wandering Minstrel. Say! How about The Melody Man?"

And that's how I became Myron Floren, the Melody
Man on KSOO.

I ended up doing two shows every day—at seven each
morning I did a music program for Nickel and Sons Harness; at noon the Gamble Stores sponsored my show.

That was the beginning of my love affair with radio—
and later with TV.

After about four weeks of the program, I asked Don,
who was doing the announcing in the morning, "How can
we tell if anyone is listening?"

"Why not give away a picture?" he suggested.

That struck me as a great idea; so the next show I mentioned casually that anyone who might like a picture
could drop a card to the station, and I would mail one out
free of charge. Three days later I received an excited call
from the secretary: "Wait till you see the mail that has
come in! There are hundreds of postcards and letters!"

I could feel my heart leap; people were really listening!
I was a success!

My days became even busier. After my morning program I had to get back to the dorm by eight to work in the

kitchen. Classes lasted until eleven-thirty, when I had to hurry back to the station to do the noon show. At one, there were more classes, followed by waiting on tables in the dining room of the dorm and studying all evening. Even then I was a real workaholic! I was also receiving many requests to do shows for service clubs, dance halls, hospitals, and even for the state prison. I was getting all the experience in entertaining that I could handle, and I loved every minute of it!

After I had finished my second year at Augustana my outside activities were taking up more and more time. To be closer to the radio station and the Carpenter and Cataract hotels where I did a lot of entertaining, I moved to the YMCA. I shared a room with Ted Lubitz, a blind piano tuner. This made my rent about three and a half dollars per week. I would buy a five dollar meal ticket at a local restaurant, which would last me a week or ten days depending on how many free meals I would be offered on the job. The five-cent bus fare from the college downtown had been eating into my resources, and walking the three blocks carrying my accordion not only saved me money but provided an extra helping of exercise.

With all that extra work, I was able to save a little money. I was astounded to realize one day that I had amassed a fortune reaching into four figures—$1,001 and change, as a matter of fact.

I decided to spend some of it on a trip to New York City to meet some of my idols in the accordion field. I figured that by carefully watching my pennies, I might be able to make the trip for around two hundred dollars, not counting train fare.

Since I had been staying in a YMCA in Sioux Falls, I decided the best place for me in New York would be Sloane House, also a YMCA hostel. Here too, rent was something

44

like three dollars and fifty cents a week. Not only was *that* within my means, but they also offered special tours at reduced prices, so I would be able to see the city without paying for taxi service everywhere I went. Most of the tours were by bus or subway at a nickel a ride.

I took a train out to Coney Island one day and tried all the rides—even a new parachute drop. The whole day set me back only four dollars and fifty cents. My companion that day was a young soldier from Iowa, so most of the ride operators wouldn't even take a fare from us.

Somehow the war in Europe seemed much closer in New York than it had in South Dakota. I saw men and women in military uniform everywhere I went!

I was determined to meet as many accordionists as possible, so I made my first stop Pietro Deiro's Accordion Headquarters in Greenwich Village. I had bought a lot of music from them in the past few years, so we all felt like we had already met. Mr. Deiro arrived by taxicab late in the afternoon on the day I had chosen for my visit. He was known as the "daddy of the piano accordion," since he had helped to develop the right hand, or treble keyboard, with the use of piano keys instead of buttons.

Pietro had been a headliner in the vaudeville circuits, and his shock of unruly white hair combined with his overall rugged appearance still gave him a commanding presence. He played some of his new numbers for me, and I, in turn, surprised him by playing many of his older compositions. It was Mr. Deiro who introduced me to Charles Magnante and Joe Biviano—two of the all-time great accordionists. Mr. Magnante was very friendly; he invited me to visit the "Lucky Strike Hit Parade" radio show, which he played every week. He told me to pay close attention to a very thin young man who would be singing on the show that afternoon.

45

"Everyone tells me that this young guy will someday be a great star," Mr. Magnante told me.

The show started with the usual fanfare, and by about the third number, many of the girls in the audience started to get very restless. I don't remember all the songs, but the one that really started things was "All or Nothing at All."

As the young man sang, the girls went wild. All over the audience they were screaming, fainting, and crying.

"Frankie, Frankie!" was the universal cry... by now I don't even have to tell you that the young man was Frank Sinatra!

One of the tours from Sloane House went to the RCA building. I was fascinated by the vast size of the operation; compared with our own little studio in Sioux Falls, RCA was enormous! I was particularly thrilled with a demonstration of something called "television." I stood on a small stage in front of a microphone and watched myself on a viewing screen about six by eight inches... my first appearance on live TV.

When I got home, I discovered that I still had twenty-one dollars left of the two hundred dollars I had allowed myself for the trip!

During my sophomore year I was approached by the Williams Piano Company to do some accordion teaching. They proposed to pay me so much for each student plus a five percent commission on any of the larger accordions that my students might buy from them. I still had a couple of hours a day that weren't filled, so I added teaching to my load.

I was new to teaching, but I felt that I knew my subject pretty well. Like all the other Williams Piano Company teachers, I canvassed Sioux Falls offering my services, and before long I had about ninety students. Some of my students came up with the idea of forming an accordion

46

band; it seemed like a good idea to me, too, so we formed groups and did a lot of extra practicing. One of the groups progressed so well that we formed a quartet that quickly became very popular at local dances, church functions, and parties. One of the favorite numbers that the quartet performed was "The Lost Chord" by Arthur Sullivan (of Gilbert and Sullivan fame), because the accordion quartet gave us an organ-like sound.

One of my first students was a pretty young sophomore from Washington High School, Berdyne Koerner. Her dad was the barber I had been going to for the few months I had been in Sioux Falls (he charged only twenty-five cents for student haircuts). I think I fell in love with her the moment I saw her.

Well, she became my student and eventually a great deal more...

World events were beginning to intrude upon our lives in South Dakota. There were many times when my noon shows were interrupted by shortwave broadcasts from Germany. The chancellor of Germany, Adolf Hitler, spoke to huge crowds that grew louder and more fanatical all the time. I couldn't understand German, but even though the words were translated into English, the power of his speeches could be felt without translation. His hypnotic harangues on the glory of the Fatherland, *Lebensraum* and the Third Reich evoked cheers of "Heil Hitler!" As the crowds cheered, I could feel cold chills running up and down my spine. Would we become involved? Would I become involved?

Toward the end of our sophomore year, Howard Hillman and I began talking about joining the newly activated United States Air Force. My earlier interest in flying had been rekindled, and we both had read about all the advantages of military service. Yes, we decided to enlist and went together for our physicals. Howard was accepted. I was turned down. I knew Dr. Opheim, the examining physician, through the Sioux Falls Kiwanis Club.

"I'm sorry, Myron," he said, "I can't pass you for flight training. You have a damaged heart valve and could never be able to perform any strenuous duties. Have you ever had any trouble with your heart?"

I assured him I had never had any problem with my heart.

"Have you had any high fevers or serious infections?" he asked next.

"Well," I replied, "I did have rheumatic fever three times when I was a kid."

"That's it," he answered. "You will never be able to do any heavy or very tiring work."

That was pretty bad news, but I figured there must be plenty of ways I could live an active life even with a heart that didn't function a hundred percent. I threw myself more and more into my work. My days began at six in the morning and continued at full tilt until midnight or even later. I accepted every job that was offered and searched for more. I especially enjoyed doing shows for hospitals and for the state prison. They taught me how really important music is for every life, especially when freedom is taken away, whether by law or by illness.

I remember a very brave young girl at Sioux Valley Hospital. Her name was Arloene Marshall, and she was hopelessly crippled. We became good friends, and I always took heart from her courageous smile and positive attitude. I gained more from these shut-in audiences than they gained from me. My music brought them a few

48

moments of carefree pleasure; their courage gave me a lifetime of inspiration.

December 7, 1941. I listened with anger and dread to the reports of the surprise attack against Pearl Harbor by the Japanese. The following day my noon show was interrupted by President Franklin Delano Roosevelt's speech declaring war on Japan. At the end of the speech, Ron Rawson, the news announcer, said, "And now back to Myron Floren, the Melody Man." Now *that* was a spot, as we say in show biz, that you wouldn't want to give to your cleaner! I had about five minutes left of the show. I don't remember what I said, but I played the national anthem and a hymn. There are times when you just don't play a polka!

The war was becoming worse every day. Inevitably the first draft call was issued, and I received my letter of "Greetings" as did most of my friends. I thought that this personal invitation from Uncle Sam might be my ticket into the Air Force, but I was wrong. When I reported for my physical, Dr. Opheim greeted me, saying, "Myron, I don't have to even examine you. They'll never accept you in the military."

At my insistence, however, we went through my physical and, sure enough, I was classified 4-F—unfit for any type of military duty.

That was really a bad blow, especially since all my friends were being accepted and leaving for duty. And uniforms were becoming a common sight around town, especially after a large air base was established nearby.

I was frequently called upon to entertain at the USO center at the air base. And that gave me the opportunity to volunteer for overseas duty through the USO office in

New York City. In just a few weeks I was interviewed, accepted, and told to be ready to leave on short notice. I was relieved and excited finally to become a part of the war against Hitler.

While awaiting my call from the USO, I busied myself with the accordion and my classes. At the same time I began to take even more notice of my favorite student, Berdyne Koerner. She was almost seventeen. Then one Sunday the Koerners invited me to a picnic; and during the afternoon, when I saw Berdyne coming toward me, her pant legs rolled above her knees, I decided then and there that I would marry her.

I finally popped the question, and the answer was, "Yes!"

I thought Berdyne would have a lot of teasing from her classmates because I was an "older" man and a *musician*. I'm sure some of them tried to persuade her to change her mind, maybe even suggesting some other more eligible man. I imagined I could hear them saying, "An accordion player? You can do better than that! Now I know this dog catcher..."

Soon we began hearing reports of boys my own age and younger in the war. There was Duke Hedman and his brave deeds with the Flying Tigers. Joe Foss of Sioux Falls was fighting in the South Pacific and becoming a national hero. And then there were the bad reports: Henry Sorenson, my friend from Roslyn, had been killed in Italy; my college roommate, Howard, who had joined the Air Force in 1939, was shot down over Germany. Gold stars signifying a death in the armed forces appeared in many windows. There were dark days ahead, and none of us would be immune from the effects of the war.

For two and a half years I continued teaching, entertaining, and waiting; teaching, entertaining, and waiting.

50

I was very confident my call would come, but I realized my name was given a very low priority because of the results of my physical exam and because I was unwilling to accept a domestic assignment.

And then in June 1944, I received orders to report to New York as soon as possible.

A "Semiprivate" Stateroom

"*Vare for sectig* ('be careful'), Myron." Pa embraced me tightly. He had a habit of lapsing into Norwegian at moments of stress.

It was an emotional farewell. Pa and Ma were usually very stoic. But I saw each of them turn aside frequently to wipe away tears.

The railroad station was crowded that morning. Groups of my friends—draftees and volunteers alike—were being directed to their railroad cars by tough-talking sergeants. "I should be in one of those groups," I thought, but fate had decreed otherwise.

My sisters were all there—all talking at once. "Take care of yourself." "Get plenty of sleep." "Eat good food; take your vitamins!" "Don't worry about us; we'll write to you."

Berdyne, my fiancée for only a few short weeks, smiled through tears. "I love you, Myron. I'll write every day, I promise."

"I love you, too, Honey," I replied. "And I'll be counting the days till we can be together forever." We hugged each other—a little self-consciously.

"Keep warm, Myron." As always, Ma was worried that I'd catch cold if I didn't bundle up.

"Don't worry. I'll keep warm, and I'll write to each of you so you'll know what I'm doing."

"All Aboaaaard!!" Our farewells were cut short.

I tried to etch each and every face into my memory through my train window. I watched my family and Berdyne until they were out of sight. Then, sinking back in my seat, I suddenly felt very much alone. So did most of the other fellows. And I realized that millions of people all over the world were going through the same upheaval. For most of us, life would never be the same again.

I had no idea where I was going, but gradually I began to recognize a strong feeling that no matter what happened for the next few months, I would be back. Even the clickety-clack of the train's wheels seemed to be repeating, "You'll be back. You'll be back."

I folded my hands and prayed for God's help and protection. The words of the Twenty-third Psalm brought confidence to my mind.

We snaked slowly out of South Dakota, through Iowa, and into Illinois. I marveled at the sight of bumper crops maturing all across the country. It seemed as if the earth knew the world was at war and was trying to do its part to help. I felt great pride in the beauty and generosity of our country.

Changing trains in Chicago started out to be a real nightmare. There were only two tracks in Sioux Falls; in Chicago there seemed to be hundreds! And wartime had multiplied the usual crowds. But everyone was pulling together to help, and in no time at all a porter directed me to the right gate, and I joined the mad rush to my car when the gate was opened.

The variety, activity, and efficiency of the towns and cities we passed through fascinated me. In later years I would become very familiar with all of them, but they were new and exciting then. I loved all of them: Gary, Indiana; Cleveland; Pittsburgh; Philadelphia; and, at last, New York! July 9, 1944.

And what a bewildering mass of people, most of whom were in uniform. Many, too, were in the uniforms of allied countries—Australia, Canada, New Zealand, and England—all gathering in New York on their way to the war zones of Europe and the South Pacific.

With accordion and suitcases, I walked the two blocks to my "hotel"—Sloane House on Thirty-fourth Street—and rented a room for five dollars a week.

When I called USO headquarters to report my arrival and location, the secretary said, "Sloane House? That's not a hotel!"

"Well," I answered, "my room has a bed, dresser, chair, and table, and a bathroom with shower is four doors down the hall. And it is only five dollars a week."

"I see what you mean," she said. "Anyhow, welcome to New York and Camp Shows. We'll call you later today with information about shots, uniforms, and travel orders. You'll find out where you are going when you get there!"

Early the next morning an Army truck picked me up at Sloane House. I met some other accordionists who were also heading for Camp Shows: Johnny Kiado from Hollywood, Carl Tatz of Providence, and Cliff Scholl from New York State. We quickly became good friends, and I surprised Johnny by playing one of his compositions.

At Saks Fifth Avenue we were fitted to uniforms. "But these are officers' uniforms," I protested to the tailor. "There must be some mistake. We're really just civilians."

"In Camp Shows, you'll be given the rank of captain," he answered. "Then if you are captured, the enemy will treat you as officers."

"That's real comforting," Johnny said, voicing my sentiments exactly.

"You can pick up your uniforms tomorrow," the tailor continued. "And God bless you for helping to entertain the boys. My son lost a leg at Anzio, so I know how important a little touch of home is over there."

Then on to a local hospital for another complete physical and the first of four shots. My heart sank when the doctor put a stethoscope to my chest and looked up at me with the all-too-familiar expression on his face.

"I can't pass you for overseas duty," he said. "The way your heart sounds, you're lucky to be walking around! The USO provides a life insurance policy for ten thousand dollars, and I just can't pass you. It would not be fair to you—or to the USO."

"Doc," I said desperately, "I just can't go home now. I'll waive the insurance if you'll just put your OK on my heart condition." Then I described my typical daily routine in Sioux Falls, and he finally agreed that since I wanted to go so badly, I could waive the insurance, and he would OK my physical.

Each day was full of activity as we received our remaining shots, got passport photos, and attended endless lectures on security, disease prevention, and wartime survival—all conditioning us mentally and physically for the transformation from a peaceful country to an active war zone. When we were issued gas masks and bedding rolls at the Brooklyn Army Base, some of my colleagues began having second thoughts—couldn't they serve at home instead of overseas? But very few decided to stay home.

56

We had been instructed not to reveal any of the information we were being given, so my letters to Berdyne and my family, which I wrote almost every day, told mostly of how much I loved them and missed them. There had been no time for sight-seeing, therefore no adventures to tell.

Finally sealed orders arrived, dated August 6. "You will be picked up at 0700 hours August 7. Be ready for an extended trip." No hints where we might be headed. Security was very tight; the less we knew the safer we would be.

Imagine me waiting at the curb the next morning with accordion, suitcases, bedroll, gas mask, knapsack, and suit bag. Certainly no one would believe I was headed for a day at Coney Island!

By midmorning our bus, now with its full load of passengers, headed to our embarkation point on the Hudson River. And there at the dock was a high ocean liner—the *Aquatania*.

"I sailed to Europe on her a few years ago," one of our fellows said very excitedly. "She's beautiful! Wait till you see the staterooms! Only two people to a room, private showers, portholes, and the most comfortable beds you ever slept on in your entire life!"

The officer at the top of the gangplank, holding what seemed like an endless manifest, checked us off and assigned our rooms. Then I found my "semiprivate stateroom." Ten of us with Camp Shows, four Air Force pilots, and a couple of other officers were assigned to the same room! The "most-comfortable beds" had been replaced by sixteen bunks stacked four high. I drew a top bunk. At least we had a "private" bathroom! If this was first class, how glad I was that I hadn't come tourist!

At breakfast the third day, the endless loading noises

57

stopped, and suddenly the ship began to move. I hurried on deck to watch the tugboats nudge our ship past Ellis Island and the Statue of Liberty toward open sea. Our adventure was about to begin!

"They tell me there are over thirty-five thousand people on board this ship," Arthur Seelig of Camp Shows said to me. "A full infantry division, thousands of service troops, nurses, hospital orderlies, and the ship's company."

Thirty-five thousand people! That was more than the population of Sioux Falls!

"I imagine we'll be joining a convoy when we get out in the Atlantic," I said to a nearby ship's officer. I remembered the newsreels I had seen of convoys crossing the Atlantic.

"No," he replied. "We'll be sailing alone." I'm sure he sensed my dismay at this news, because he continued, "Don't worry, we can travel twice as fast as any of the German U-boats. And we have ways of knowing when they are in the area."

"Then why all those big cannon and antiaircraft guns on the ship?" I just had to ask.

"Well, those are just in case a U-boat slips up on us or we are attacked by fighter planes when we get closer to our destination."

Rules on board ship were necessarily strict, and penalties for breaking the rules were severe. We even heard of fellows being court-martialed for smoking on deck at night, since the glow of a single cigarette could be seen for miles at sea.

Each night the USO performers put on shows for all personnel in the main ballroom where, if they were packed like sardines, two thousand could be seated at a time. After one of the girls sang Irving Berlin's song

"How Deep Is the Ocean?" to thunderous applause, I learned that her husband, a pilot, was missing in action over Germany.

Because we were sailing in a southeasterly direction, rumor had it that we were headed for the Panama Canal and the South Pacific. The rumor was soon squelched when we turned north into rough seas and cold weather. But my Viking blood must have been stirred, because I loved to stand on the deck watching the waves break over the bow.

Lifeboat drills were held over and over until we could get to our stations in seconds—even in our sleep! The fifth afternoon we were surprised by an extra lifeboat drill. As we reached our stations we sensed trouble. All the big guns were manned and aimed at another ship in the distance until it passed and was well out of sight. Even friendly ships had to be checked out, and troops had to be protected.

For an entire week the weather remained cloudy and dreary, and the sea was continually rough. A sense of desperation seemed to pervade the ship.

Then came news that our destination would be Scotland, and that we were now within reach of land-based German bombers. Everyone became noticeably quieter as we entered the actual war zone.

The chaplains on board had never had such good attendance back in their home towns as they had on this ship. One of my roommates, a fighter pilot, told me that although he had been raised without any religious training, he now attended every service he could find. "You know," he said one evening after he had attended Protestant, Jewish, and Catholic services, "when I'm up in that little plane, I figure I need all the help I can get! And besides, deep down, all these different chaplains are telling me the same thing—God loves me and will stay by my side no matter what!"

That night I dreamed of a thunderstorm back home. I saw lightning strike a telephone pole near our house. It was midnight and pitch dark except for the flashes of lightning. In each flash it seemed as if I could see God's face as He smiled at me. As the storm passed, I began to understand that I would come home safely from this war and that He had some special purpose for me that I would discover later. With that thought, I saw a beautiful full moon come from behind a cloud. I had never felt such peace before.

ETO*

I woke at about four in the morning with a feeling of dread that comes with stillness, for the rolling of the ship and the sounds of engines had ceased. During the next twelve months, I would experience this same dread of sudden silence many times; it is a part of the thunderous shellfire and bombings and can be just as terrifying.

But this time there were no bombings and no shellfire.

When dawn broke, from my porthole I could see a most beautiful sight—the Firth of Clyde in lovely southwest Scotland, and on its bank a hillside village set against the greenest green I had ever seen.

Already boats were plying back and forth between the ship and shore—boats loaded with soldiers, guns, and equipment for war, and boats loaded with huge boxes marked "Medical Supplies and Equipment." These two extremes spoke silently and ironically of why we were here.

It was late in the day when USO replacements went ashore. Entering a train compartment directly from a door on the side was a new experience, and even though I was loaded with my accordion, bedroll, gas mask, suitcase,

*European theater of operations

knapsack, and helmet, I was eventually successful in finding a compartment with room to settle down.

But there was excitement in the air; here we were in Scotland and on our way to London. All night long, no one thought of sleep.

August 15, 1944—London!

And London was being bombarded with V-1 bombs, more popularly known as buzz bombs. Each of these small bombs resembled a small airplane with a rocket motor on the back, but actually it was a long, thin bomb with wings, a tail, and a motor spouting fire. Its sound reminded me of a Model T having trouble getting up a hill. I was soon to learn that contrary to Hitler's belief that these bombs would terrorize and kill the English people to the point of England's surrender, each one seemed only to strengthen the determination of the English to win the war.

The Army truck that met us delivered us safely to our headquarters for assignments to billets, processing, and briefings.

I was fortunate to be assigned to a home on London's north side near Regent's Park. From my third-story room I was close to a hatch through which I could crawl to the roof to watch the buzz bombs when the sirens gave warning of their approach. In the daytime, flags signaled us to take cover when the bombs came in our direction; at night the tail glow of the bomb described its path.

In spite of war, there was an excitement about being in London. Here I was in the very London I had read about and dreamed about, London with its famous buildings and parks, a pivot of world events down through the ages. And though destruction was everywhere, I had to see as much of London as I could: Number 10 Downing Street, the home of the prime minister—now the great Churchill—and one of his war offices; Marble Arch, which had received a direct hit the night I arrived but was still a place where anyone with a gripe could mount a soapbox and get a load off his mind without being bothered by police or civilians; Regent's Park; and other places of history.

But we had come to Europe to entertain and lift the spirits of our soldiers, to help them forget for a few moments the dangers and perils of war. And we looked forward to our first assignment at a U.S. Army base outside of London. Here I learned for the first time the power my accordion and I had to reach into the hearts and feelings of our men. No sooner was I introduced than all lights went out and an air raid sounded. At first we listened in silence to the planes overhead—then the antiaircraft fire. But I started to play, then asked for requests.

"'Lili Marlene!'" someone shouted.

"I don't know that. Sing it for me," I replied. Almost immediately a thousand voices commenced singing the song as if on cue. For over an hour the war was only a background to our festivities. The interval between songs was punctuated by the sound of bombs, airplane motors, and antiaircraft fire. Once in a while a bomb larger than the others would shake the building, and the singing just became louder. A special comradeship developed.

The emotions of these moments was telling me much, and I admit that tears flowed freely as I listened to these young, strong voices, so full of life and hope, yet overwhelmed with the thought that they might never see home again. It was fitting that our final song was "God Be with You Till We Meet Again," sung in a way that I can recall to this day as vividly as the night I accompanied their singing.

Omaha Beach

August 23, 1944. The headlines read, "PARIS FREED!"

That same morning our USO unit received travel orders to have breakfast and be ready to leave our billets at four the next morning for transfer to the Continent.

The tarp of our two-ton Army truck concealed us as we left London, and in about two hours we were at a pier on the south shore of England. There was our transportation to France—an LST!*

A couple of jeeps were already aboard as well as hundreds of GIs who were swarming over the ship. Our USO group was the last to arrive, and no sooner were we loaded than we heard "Cast off!" We were on our way to France.

As we gradually put out to sea, we could see other boats embarking and still others returning from the invasion area. We moved very slowly in a wide arc across the English Channel. I saw many of the soldiers searching their English/French dictionaries for words to greet the French people, the easiest phrase being, of course, "Parlez-vous français?"

*Landing ship tank

Most of the soldiers on the LST were infantrymen. The extreme seriousness of their mission was written on their faces; yet they joked and made idle conversation for relief. This seemed like a proper time for me to bring out the accordion, and we ended up singing our way to France. One song, "Mademoiselle from Armentiers," had been sung by the fathers of some of these boys on their way to the battlefields of World War I.

Silence settled in as we saw the first signs of Omaha Beach, still littered with wrecked boats and the machines of war. Mammoth iron spikes protruded from the water, "impenetrable" barricades that had been set up by the Nazis to prevent Allied landing boats from reaching shore.

Although night was coming on, we could see the cliffs above Omaha Beach with cannons sticking out of their bombed-out gun emplacements.

Finally we reached shore and were told that this beach strewn with barbed wire and other wreckage would be our camp until morning. We were reminded of the bravery and heroism that had taken place on this very spot only a few weeks before.

I have been in many places in my life where I have felt lonely, but not one compares with the loneliness of Omaha Beach—a veritable monument to loneliness.

We unpacked our bedding rolls and prepared for the night but not before "dining" on our supper K rations. I still find it hard to believe that a box the size of a Cracker Jack box can contain all the nutrients necessary to sustain life and provide body energy for an active soldier, but that is what K rations are supposed to do. Since fires would have marked us as an enemy target, we made soup with cold water from our canteens. And for dessert, a chocolate bar. At last we stretched out under the skies of France, listening to the bombardment of German troops on some offshore islands.

"What a long way from the farm in South Dakota!" I thought.

And I wondered what Dad, Mom, and my sisters and brothers were doing. And Berdyne. What would she be doing at this time of day back home? I had heard that one of her cousins had been killed in the first Allied landing in France. Could it have been on this very spot where I lay? With a deepening sense of loneliness, I rose and strained my eyes to write her a letter I would mail somewhere the next day. But months later I learned that the only part of it that got past the censors was "Dearest Berdyne" and "Lovingly Yours."

As darkness settled down, I watched the stars appearing here and there among the clouds directly overhead. And suddenly the dreadful homesickness began to lift; I could see something I had seen so many times on the farm, my old friends the Milky Way, the Big Dipper, and Orion. As a child I had spent many long summer evenings watching the stars, and as usual their great beauty made me feel closer to God and more protected than ever.

I could hear Pa reading the Twenty-third Psalm back when I had been so sick in high school. The memory lulled me to sleep, and as I drifted off, I added a small prayer of my own: "Lord, protect me through the days to come—but more than that, please guard my loved ones at home."

The Hank Ladd Show

Early the next morning a unit of Army Special Services drove us to the first of hundreds of temporary camps I would see as we headed across Europe. Here and there huge gaps appeared in hedgerows where tanks and bulldozers had made their own roads.

At this camp the next day I was introduced to my first USO unit—the Hank Ladd Show, consisting of the very funny Hank Ladd; his wife Francetta, who was a wonderful singer and Hank's foil; Johnny Barnes, a tap dancer (or "hoofer" as he liked to be called) from Washington, D.C.; and a cute young contortionist named Meribeth Old from Chanute, Kansas. She used the stage name of Brucetta. I would play background music and also do a few solo numbers on the accordion.

Following an all-morning rehearsal, we went out to an improvised stage opposite hundreds of GIs sitting in the field to watch our first show together.

I wondered if they enjoyed watching it as much as I enjoyed performing for them. By the amount of applause, I think they did.

After we had done a number of shows there, we moved on to Le Mans. Our billets were in a typical French hostel. I shared my second-story room with Johnny Morgan, later to become famous with Spike Jones, and the writer of many popular songs. Johnny was a fine banjo player even though at that time he had not learned to read music. I helped him write the notes to some of his melodies; one became "Hey, Mr. Banjo."

I loved the camaraderie of the performers. The second night at the hotel we were surprised by a visit from Dinah Shore and Paul Winchell with his wooden sidekick, Jerry Mahoney. We spent the evening telling stories and joking and having a great time, but Jerry had to be retired to his suitcase when he became a little unruly!

Special Services picked us up the next morning, and we headed for our show of the day. It was quite some distance, and we were aware of scattered pockets of resistance here and there. As we neared our destination, we noticed GIs in trenches. Suddenly a sergeant called out, "What in the world are you doing here? There are Germans all over the place!"

We had taken a wrong turn, and when our driver finally realized the danger we were in, he went through some maneuvers with that two-ton truck that I'm sure surprised the Germans even more than it surprised us. While some of the soldiers were laughing at us, others just stared in utter disbelief at the truck and its gyrations. And there I was, hanging on to my accordion with one hand and a side of the truck with the other—the original "white knuckle" rider! The only thought I remember clearly: "Where would I get another accordion if the Germans shot a hole in this one?"

Luckily, no shots were fired as we hauled out of there and found the right turn. Once headed in the right direction, we soon reached our show area for the afternoon, although we were somewhat subdued by afterfright.

Then, as now, every show gave me something to remember. Especially memorable are the ones where the audiences are with the performers all the way. The rapport between performers and audience becomes a sort of short-lived love affair. I have done shows where I felt I have not lived up to the expectations of the audience—and many more when I have not lived up to my own expectations. Berdyne tells me that even now she knows whether or not I feel I have done a good show by my mood upon entering our home after a day of TV shows or a trip out of town. On the bad days I don't have to say a word; even before I see her, I'll hear her say, "Okay, what went wrong today?" And I can still hear Pa and Ma say, "Don't cry over spilled milk. It's done and can't be undone." Even so, I try to analyze what went wrong to avoid the same problem another time.

The Allied front was moving swiftly. Our next move was to Paris!

On September 7, at the head of a division of American troops, we entered Paris somewhere west of the Arc de Triomphe and turned onto the Champs Elysées to a scene that is burned into my memory—the Champs Elysées was the *widest* street I had ever seen!

And the glow of deliverance was still shining on the faces of the French people.

I rode on the hood of an Army jeep. Pretty girls (and *all* the girls in Paris were pretty!) would run up with wine, cookies, hugs, kisses, and welcoming shouts: "America, we love you!"; *"Vive la France!"*; and *"Vive l'Américain!"* I felt very proud and privileged to be in France when our two countries were so close and loyal in spirit.

Our Army vehicles were smothered by the thousands of French on bicycles, and here and there we'd pass a French truck with a stove on one back corner burning wood or charcoal for fuel. In 1944, a possible solution to our gasoline shortage today!

Special Services had billeted us at the Hôtel Georges V. It was the most elegant hotel I had ever seen—in fact, I don't think that I have seen one yet to rival it in beauty and grace. Our orders were to relax and rest for a few days.

Relax? I had to see Paris!

I became a typical tourist. My first stop was the famous Paris Opera. From my seat in the back I watched the opera company perform *Thäis*. I noticed that many young Frenchmen nearby had complete scores of the opera and were following it note by note.

Everywhere I went I would find GIs with the same thought—see and do as much as possible. Because it had been declared an open city, Paris had not been bombed; that wonderful city of culture had been left virtually untouched. I visited Nôtre Dame, the Louvre, the Place de la Concorde, and the Sorbonne. The statues amazed me; I could easily imagine the years of toil that went into each one of them. Much of the magnificent artwork, for which Paris is so famous, had been hidden from the Germans, but enough remained to impress a visitor from South Dakota!

The traffic circle around the Arc de Triomphe was constantly jammed with every kind of motor vehicle imaginable. Crossing it was a major undertaking, made even more frightening to this particular young country boy by drivers who relied more on their horns than on their brakes!

One day while riding in the subway, I decided to try my French and spoke to a prosperous-looking gentleman sitting across from me. "*Il fait beaujour aujour d'hui, n'est-ce pas?*" I said.

"Yes," he replied in English considerably more understandable than my high school French, "It is a *very* beautiful day!"

The gentleman went on to explain that he was a teacher of English at the University of Paris. Learning that I was part of an entertainment unit he asked if I would join him, his wife and two daughters for dinner.

"Bring a friend," he added. So Johnny Barnes and I went to his lovely home in St. Germaine on the outskirts of Paris. They told us many stories of their lives under the Germans. I had noticed signs painted on front doors, "*Bien Italien.*" Questioned about these signs, the professor explained that after the liberation, families of Italian extraction who were known *not* to have supported the invading Germans were recognized so no reprisals would be taken by the local Free French forces.

Several weeks later our base was moved to St.-Dizier. There we stayed in a small hotel in the center of town. I was in the habit of practicing the accordion for an hour or so each morning before we left for shows. One morning, from my second-floor room I noticed a group of civilians starting to gather across the narrow street in front of the hotel. I stepped closer to the window to see what was happening and was surprised when I realized they were listening to my music! The curtain prevented them from seeing me, so I walked back to the bed and sat down and continued my practice session. For some reason I had thought that only American soldiers would be listening to my music, but here were French people of all ages straining to hear me. Of course I played a little louder as the crowd grew.

When I finished my usual numbers, I decided to thank them for the compliment of their attention by playing the

French national anthem, "La Marseillaise." At the first strain, I could feel the electricity building; within a few seconds the entire crowd had begun to sing, softly at first, then louder as if they suddenly realized they were once again free to sing their beloved national song. As I neared the end of the anthem, I walked to the window and pushed the curtain aside; there I discovered Claude Singleton, our driver, conducting the impromptu chorus. Emotion caught me, and tears began to roll down the bellows of the accordion, but mine were not the only tears in the gathering! At the last note, I bowed slightly and gave the "V for victory" sign.

With the swiftly changing battlefront and with the German army falling back toward the Siegfried Line, our next location was to be Eupen, Belgium, near the German city of Aachen. Aachen was under heavy siege by the Allied forces.

As we headed north from Paris, Hank Ladd opened a top-secret communique. He read:

> You are entering an active war zone and extra precautions must be taken to ensure your safety. Under no circumstances are you to talk to or fraternize with any German civilians. Do not pick up souvenirs. Lugers, helmets, bayonets, etc., may be booby trapped. Death or dismemberment could result.

Needless to say, we followed those instructions to the letter!

It was late afternoon when we arrived in Eupen and found our billets in an old monastery outside of town. I unrolled my bedroll on the top floor and was just settling down to reread letters from Berdyne and my sister

Virginia when the building began to vibrate. I ran to the window and looked out. A red glow was approaching from the east. It was a buzz bomb—and this one was low! As it approached, its fiendish outline became starkly clear. It looked as if it would hit the building just where I was standing!

Just then Johnny came running into the room with his helmet pulled down tight over his ears. "What are you doing here?" he shouted. "Get downstairs at once!"

I turned for one more look just in time to see the bomb shoot past us and continue on its way to England—just barely missing our roof!

Johnny and I walked shakily down the stairs, where we were surprised to see a young GI sitting calmly on the last step, writing a letter. He looked up and grinned: "You'll see a lot of those little rockets around here. The launching site is just a bit east of here. You'll get used to it."

Somehow I doubted that!

Hank, Francetta, Meribeth, and Johnny had been in England and on the Continent for more than three years. Now it was finally time for them to return home for a very well earned rest. Our next trip into Paris would be our last time together, and I would be assigned to a new show.

The Don Rice Show

"I'm Don Rice, this is Phyllis 'P.J.' Clever from Youngstown, Ohio, Sandy Rozell from Winthrop, Massachusetts, and Kitty Barret of London. I hear you're from South Dakota; that makes us neighbors—I'm from Waukon, Iowa. Ever hear of it?"

"No, can't say that I have," I answered, "but one of these days I'll probably play there. Anyway, it's nice meeting you all. I'm happy to be with your show."

"Glad to have you," Don said. "We call our show Fun Marches On! I do comedy; Kitty is my 'straight man': P.J. sings; and Sandy does a Scotch act in kilts and combat boots. He plays a 'fish horn' (straight soprano saxophone). You'll do background music and also a couple of solo numbers on each show."

I shook hands with each of them. Phyllis was pretty, blond, and vivacious. Kitty was a beautiful brunette with all her curves in the right places.

"Kitty," I said, "I hope you don't mind my saying that you look less like a 'straight man' than anyone I have ever seen! And Sandy, I'll bet you have a lot of stories to tell."

Sandy was a Scotsman whose once-red hair was now nearly all gray. At sixty plus, he was about five feet eight inches of mischievous twinkle. His face was a map of his frequently rough life in show business; both good and bad breaks of the past fifty years showed clearly. He said as he shook my hand, "Aye, laddie, I do have a lot of stories to tell, and someday you'll have a lot of your own."

"Why do you wear combat boots with your outfit? Doesn't the audience laugh when you come out like that?"

"Yes, they surely do," Sandy replied. "And that's exactly why I wear them—to get that little extra snicker. One of the tricks of the trade. You'll see."

"Sandy forgot his shoes at one of our first shows," Don added. "So he had to wear the combat boots. It got such a big laugh that we decided to leave it in."

I've discovered since then that *that* is the very best way to build an act.

Our three-hour rehearsal that afternoon in Chatou on the outskirts of Paris was a good beginning of friendships that lasted the next nine months and are still continuing today!

Afterward we were introduced to Severino Barba of Milwaukee, the man assigned to be our driver. He had come to Europe with the infantry but had shot off half of his trigger finger in a freak accident and had been assigned to Special Services. Sergeant Barba was short, stocky, and dark complected; there was always a smile on his face.

"Glad to meet you all," he said happily. "We're gonna have a wonderful time."

"Barb" was certainly true to his word. I can't remember any time during our nine months together that he didn't solve whatever problems came up with a smile and an encouraging word. I saw him a few years ago in Milwaukee, and he still had that same happy disposition.

We were not scheduled to leave Chatou for Holland until the end of the week, so we had Thanksgiving Day off. Sandy and I decided to go into Paris for dinner at the enlisted men's mess. The countryside and falling snow reminded me so much of home that to avoid an attack of homesickness I concentrated on the dinner we were to enjoy. *Stars and Stripes,* the Army newspaper, had reported that every American fighting person would have turkey with all the trimmings for the holiday meal. Ever since Omaha Beach, we had lived on K rations and C rations, so the promise of home-style cooking gave us the incentive to walk for our dinner.

The 350 GIs crowded into the dining hall were looking forward to a real meal too, but not before an Army chaplain offered a prayer of special thanksgiving, ending with a heartfelt plea for peace and for the safety of all our soldiers. I can't remember a more eloquent prayer or a more satisfying meal!

And next morning, on to Maastricht, Holland, our base for the next series of shows. While we would eat in an Army mess, we would be billeted at 44 Stationstrat, the home of the Charles Samperman family.

Surrounded by their six children, I felt very much at home right away! One of their daughters now lives in California.

"You are welcome to our home. What we have is yours for as long as you stay," Mr. Samperman greeted us. Communication was easy—they, with a little English, were also able to understand my Norwegian.

After our first show the next night, I wrote in my diary, "Show a smash hit!" And it certainly was a smash hit for *me;* I was on stage the whole time and loved it!

General William Simpson, commander of the Ninth Army was there. His very presence commanded respect. And his six feet four inches, with ramrod-straight stance, made him the Texan that he was, and reminded me of the type of officer Randolph Scott would portray in the movies. Besides being our very good friend, he honored us by making our troupe the official show attached to the Ninth Army. I still have the Ninth Army patch on my USO uniform (which still fits, by the way!). Recently I had the great pleasure of dining with General Simpson at his San Antonio home and reminiscing about those busy, exciting days.

We couldn't help but notice the increasing activity in our sector of the front. We were doing more and more shows in areas that seemed to be part of the active war zone. The "Red Ball Express," Army Supply, was everywhere, and mountains of supplies, fuel, and ammunition were being amassed. Occasionally a German shell would hit one of these supply dumps, and the fire would burn for days.

Our entertainment schedule took us through all sorts of bad roads and weather, and we were ever thankful for the four-wheel drive on both the jeep and the truck. I generally rode "shotgun," looking for road signs while Barb drove. I can still see his look of fiendish glee when he would spot some especially hazardous stretch where the heavy armament had pounded the road into a mud lake. He would throw the jeep into four-wheel drive, holler "Geronimo!!" and plunge straight through the low spots. Many times I could have scooped up handfuls of mud just by sticking my hand out the window!

To cut down on travel time, we were moved to a small hostel in Heerlen, much nearer the actual fighting. From there we were able to do extra shows every day. Even so, our shows had to be done during daylight hours. Travel after dark was not allowed.

Intelligence information about new advances in Nazi weaponry had created an urgency to get a new push started. After one of our shows, an officer was talking

1. The station square at Heerlen, the Netherlands, during peaceful times.

2. My long-hair period at three years.

3. Getting my feet wet. The mud felt so good between my toes!

4. (*Right*) As Big Brother, I show Arlie how machinery is put together. Notice the family car in the background.

5. (*Below*) This was the main street in Roslyn. Valborg, Mother, Genevieve, Arlie, and me with our new 1926 Essex parked beside the pump at Rasmussen's filling station.

6. (*Below*) An early picture of the Floren brothers and sisters. L–R: Valborg, Virginia, me with my original "button box," Duane, Gloria, Genevieve, and Arlie. That's Jack in the lower right with his tongue hanging out.

7. (*Above*) A later picture of the Floren brothers and sisters. Next to me in my sporting white slacks is Arlie; then Valborg, Genevieve, Virginia, Gloria, and Duane (also called "Dewey").

8. (*Below*) How proud my parents were of their family. L–R: Genevieve and Gloria on each side of me, then Arlie and Valborg. Seated: Virginia, Dad (Ole), Mom (Tillie), and Duane in his Marine uniform. *Photo by Harold.*

9. The Ole and Tillie Floren farm in Roslyn, South Dakota, about 1920. Uncle Olaf's farm buildings are in the background.

10. This is the spot in Roslyn where our house stood before it was moved to Webster.

11. And here is the original house after it was moved to Webster.

12. Mom and Pa in front of the Webster High School about 1938.

13. Here I am with my second piano-accordion. Was I ever one lucky person!

14. There was room in this picture for only half of the students of the Floren Accordion Studios, Sioux Falls, 1941.

15. My Sioux Falls accordion band—the first in South Dakota. Lois Berven, my secretary and assistant teacher, is standing next to me. In the front row left is Berdyne Koerner, later to become Mrs. Myron Floren.

16. This was my first publicity give-away picture when I was at Augustana College and working at KSOO.

17. The "Melody Man" about 1943.

18. (*Above*) Webster's Booster Band. Notice the accordion in the back row just to the right of the big horn. Do you recognize who is holding it?

19. (*Below*) Here I am in my USO uniform at the Sloane House YMCA in New York as I await orders to ship out to the ETO.

20. This is what Paris does; it puts a big smile on your face. 1945.
Photo by Harcourt, Paris.

21. This big smile belongs to Severino Barba (known as "Barb"). He was our driver with Special Services in the ETO.

22. (*Below left*) This ETO snapshot gives good advice throughout life.
23. (*Below right*) During the war many cars and trucks in France had wood burners attached to generate methane fuel since gasoline was not available.

24. (*Above*) Here I am in my field uniform with my "best friend," ready to set out for a day of entertaining wounded patients in ETO evacuation hospitals.

25. (*Below*) Claude Singleton, our driver for the Hank Ladd Show, with his truck and trailer, typical USO transportation.

26. A wonderful friend—Don Rice of the Don Rice USO show.
Photo by James Kriegsmann, N.Y.

27. (*Above*) Members of the Don Rice Show: Sandy, P.J., the Accordion Man, Kitty, and Don Rice.

28. (*Left*) Members of the Don Rice Show somewhere in Holland.

29. (*Below*) The Don Rice cast with General Simpson (seated between Kitty and P.J.) and his staff at the 9th Army Headquarters in Holland.

30. (*Left*) This is the hotel Niederlandischer Hof in Schwerin, where I first met GI Joe.

31. (*Below*) August 19, 1945 at the First Lutheran Church in Sioux Falls.

about a German jet fighter that had been shot down; it was being dismantled to be shipped back to the States for study. According to our pilots, the speed of those jets was amazing, and they were worried about further development.

As we listened, a sergeant excitedly called us to the door. "Look at that jagged cloud trail," he said as he pointed toward the north. "That's the new V-2. You can't see or hear them, and you never know where they will land. They're being aimed at London and Amsterdam." The buzz bombs (V-1s) and V-2s were the crude beginnings of our jet planes and space travel.

With Christmas fast approaching, our shows were more in demand than ever. The weather became wintry—clouds and constant rain. And the high level of bombing grew heavier each day.

The Nazis were reportedly reeling on every front when, with shocking suddenness, the area south of us was overrun by thousands of German soldiers, tanks, and artillery. They broke through our positions south of Aachen on a wide front; their objective was to cut the Allied armies in two with a drive to the sea. For days they advanced at will, the cloudy winter weather allowing them to advance with no danger from our air force.

The morning of the breakthrough, some of the other shows talked of going back to Paris.

Don and I talked it over with the other members of our troupe and decided to wait till we received further orders from General Simpson's headquarters. Shortly thereafter word came through that although the situation looked serious, the general was sure it would be contained very soon. We decided to stay; after all, our soldiers would need entertainment now more than ever!

A few days into what became known as the Battle of the Bulge, a group under General McAuliffe was surrounded in Bastogne. The general's reply to the German order to surrender gave a much-needed shot in the arm to the morale of our troops. His response was the now famous "Nuts!"

The bombing of Heerlen appeared to be the last gasp of the dying German air force. The bombing may have succeeded in turning the war to their advantage earlier, but the weather finally cleared and allowed the Allied air armadas to take to the skies once again. We watched in awe as thousands of fighters and bombers converged over Heerlen and then fanned out for their strikes over Germany. We could see enemy antiaircraft flak bursting in the sky, we were so close to the battle. Late in the afternoon our planes began to return to their bases. Now and then a bomber would be flying very close to the ground with smoke trailing behind and three or four fighters flying protective cover like anxious mother hens. The strength of our air force combined with their shortage of fuel and ammunition finally stalled the German advance, and they retreated to their original battle lines within Germany.

On one of our trips to the front, I met Major Rex Hays with the Second Armored Division. Rex had offered me my first job at WNAX in Yankton a few years earlier while I was still in Webster High School. (He is currently head of the musicians' union in Yankton.) And I noticed that many of the soldiers who had gathered for the show were weighted down with extra ammunition, and many were carrying hand grenades. It made me wonder what bad news they had heard about our show! I cautioned them to sit down very carefully. Just then a Special Services lieutenant spoke to me quietly. "Please. Do the best show

82

you ever did. We're heading into an important battle tonight, and many of us probably won't be back."

I remember those three shows as some of the warmest and best we had ever done. I couldn't have asked for more responsive audiences as we finished each program with "God Be with You."

The same officer came backstage after the last show, thanked us all, and then said, "If you want to see a sight you'll never forget, look toward the east at three tomorrow morning."

Back in Heerlen, I set my alarm and fell asleep with the faces of those men swirling in my mind. At exactly three, Don and I watched the whole eastern horizon as it lit up like one gigantic flash of lightning ... the thunder of thousands of guns reached us a few seconds later.

We prayed for the young men we had entertained that afternoon, and I thought, "If I hadn't had rheumatic fever when I was fourteen, I might have been part of that battle!"

Later the next afternoon we heard that our troops had been successful in crossing the Roer River into Germany.

As the Army poured across the Roer and then the Rhine into Germany for the last big assault of the war, we USO people continued to do our daily shows. After one particularly busy day, we were having coffee at an advanced command post when Jimmy Morello, our Special Services representative, walked in with a beautiful lady on his arm.

She walked up to me, extending her hand for a firm handshake, and said, "Hello, Myron. I've heard so much about you. I'm Marlene Dietrich."

She had heard about *me*?! I was speechless!

Later we met Lily Pons and Andre Kostelanetz at Krefeld; how the GIs loved them! They joined us for a show for the Eighty-third Division at Neuss and again in Düsseldorf.

Occasionally we went to advance posts on the west bank of the Rhine River, where we could see German cities on the eastern side, still under German control, being assaulted by one thunderous bombardment after another. But on the last day of March, our little USO troupe was driven across the Rhine on a pontoon bridge built by the Army Corps of Engineers. The bridge was made of huge rafts tied side by side to form a single lane for traffic; the rafts rested on big empty oil drums. Today I think of that crossing whenever the traffic is especially heavy on the Los Angeles freeways! My memory of the cities of the Ruhr Valley is of mountains of rubble—not one building was standing.

In early April we were ordered back to the USO base at Chatou. One morning I decided to walk into Paris to mail some letters and do a little sight-seeing. I was greeted by flags at half staff and by tearful Frenchmen who would run up and embrace me, expressing sympathy at my loss. I rushed to a newsstand to discover the reason. President Roosevelt was dead! "Impossible," I thought. "What a terrible irony that he should die when victory is so close."

The whole world felt this shock. All over Paris people wore black armbands and mourned the loss of a great leader. Harry Truman summed up our feelings best when he said, "I feel as though a load of hay had been dropped on me!"

Northern Germany
and GI Joe

Our next assignment took us to the Mecklenberg region of northern Germany. We were to live for a while in Schwerin near the Baltic Sea.

Every road was crowded with endless lines of DPs*— German men, women, and children on their way home after fleeing to the countryside during the bombings of the previous weeks. Some of the more fortunate people rode bicycles with the handlebars and racks piled high with their remaining precious personal possessions. Others pulled carts or pushed wheelbarrows.

The massive bombings had left the towns and cities devastated. For most, home would be a solitary, bombed-out shell. A lucky few who still had houses would find they had been stripped of their furnishings. What a sharp contrast to the beautiful, almost undisturbed rural countryside!

Occasionally we traveled by way of the German *Autobahn*—beautiful ribbons of superhighway that criss-

*Displaced persons

crossed the "fatherland." Hitler had had the roads built to speed the movement of troops. I wonder if the *autobahns* gave President Eisenhower the inspiration to build our own incredible system of interstate highways?

On May 8, 1945 we received the news we had all been praying for; Germany had surrendered to the Allies! The show we did that evening in Schwerin was the happiest and most successful of the entire tour.

The clean, picturesque city of Schwerin was like another planet. For some reason, it had been spared the trauma of bombings. As we drove into town, we saw many old German women on their hands and knees scrubbing the steps in front of their homes; a few glanced up at us in mute resignation. I wondered how many of them had lost loved ones in the recent battles. They looked so much like the women of South Dakota that I found it difficult to look at them without terrible pangs of homesickness.

After a little searching we finally pulled to a stop in front of the small hostel we were to live in. I was about to open the door of the hostel when it seemed to swing open all by itself. Surprised, I found myself staring at a boy who seemed to be about 15 years old. He was dressed in over-sized Army fatigues and had the widest grin I had ever seen.

"Welcome, Amerikaner!" he said proudly, "Me, GI Joe. This is your hotel. I take care of you!"

I looked closer at our host; he was about five feet six inches tall and very, very thin. His curly dark hair looked as if it had never felt the touch of a comb. His face was young, but his eyes seemed ancient. He ushered us into the hotel and clapped his hands, and a half dozen assorted bellmen, maids, office boys, and porters—all German—appeared as if by magic, and he instructed them to gather our bags and carry them to our rooms. GI Joe grabbed my suitcases and accordion and led me to my second-floor room. The window facing the east overlooked a beautiful, small lake. I noticed a feather comforter on the bed. Joe wondered if that would be enough to keep me warm; after all, it got pretty cold this far north at night. I assured him it would be fine; in fact, it was the lightest and coziest cover I had enjoyed in many months! After a bath in a real bathtub and a light dinner in the hotel dining room, I settled down to what I expected to be a really good night's sleep. But Joe's haunted eyes kept floating above me and I resolved to learn more about him and help him if I possibly could.

The following evening the soldiers billeted in the hostel gathered in the lobby area for an impromptu show. We passed a few stories around and then I got my accordion out so we could sing a few songs. The evening passed quickly as we sang song after song in English, French, even German; until finally one of the soldiers said to Joe, "Come on, kid. Sing your favorite song for us." (Joe had already become the company's adopted child.)

Joe started singing and I joined in quickly with the accordion. He sang, "My Yiddishe Mama." I had never heard that song before, but found that for some reason, I could play it perfectly. No one applauded at the end of the song. Joe still had the same wide grin, but now it was frozen and washed with tears. I looked around the room; there was not a dry eye in the place. All of our thoughts were with Joe, and with our families and sweethearts back home. Most of us would soon see our loved ones again—but not GI Joe.

Joe, his brother, and parents had come from Lithuania. They were a close-knit, loving Jewish family. As part of Hitler's insane plan to exterminate the Jewish people, Joe and his family were rounded up and transferred to work

87

camps in Germany. They were first sent to Auschwitz, then to Buchenwald. As the world was to discover, too late, these weren't work camps at all, but rather, extermination camps. The Jews, along with any other groups of people that Hitler had declared "sub-human," were being systematically slaughtered. New trainloads of workers poured into the camp daily, but Joe noticed that the population never really seemed to grow, and there was no particular kind of work being done.

The day finally came when Joe's parents were called to join the "workers." Joe and his brother could see that this work force was digging a deep ditch with the help of bulldozers. When the Nazi guards judged that the ditch was deep enough, fifty people were forced to strip and line up alongside it. As the boys watched, German machine gunners opened fire; all fifty people fell into the ditch as they were shot. Afterwards a few were still alive; a single bullet would then be used to end each of those lives as well. Soon Joe's parents entered the line.

Joe watched from the barracks window. *This can't be happening,* he thought, *I'm having a nightmare! Soon I'll wake and I'll be back at home; we'll all be together again!*

For a moment Joe's parents glanced at their sons; even in their despair, there was still compassion and hope in their eyes. Joe screamed and ran for the door, but his cries of rage and grief were cut short by the chatter of machine gun fire. Fifty more Jewish mothers and fathers had been killed—their last breaths hung in the cold air as their bodies fell backward.

In the silence that followed, both brothers were sick with shock and disbelief. Other prisoners gathered around them offering solace. But there was no way to help; no words could ease their pain. Much later, exhaustion finally forced Joe and his brother into the welcome oblivion of sleep. Joe dreamed of peaceful fields and a home without war.

Weeks, or possibly months, later the boys were moved to a new concentration camp at Ludwigslust. There, rumors were flying that liberation was at hand. Activity increased at the camp; more and more prisoners were arriving at the camp every day. Suddenly one morning, all the guards had vanished and Joe heard the sound of tanks approaching! He had heard tanks many times before, but these sounds were different. He could hear happy shouts of, "Freedom! Freedom! Freedom!"

The lead tank driver had spotted the camp and inspected the locked gates. Seeing the pitiful prisoners inside the fence, he decided that the time for locks was over, and proceeded to crash his tank straight through the gates and into the camp. Both he and his tank were surrounded immediately by deliriously happy prisoners.

Fifteen-year-old Joe and his brother, twenty, left the camp with the intention of returning to Lithuania to try to find any relatives who may have been spared. But Joe decided to try instead to make a new life for himself in another country and wanted to wait for the Americans, who he was sure could help him. He said goodbye to his brother, and walked into the hostel where we had found him.

"I just told all those Germans that I was taking over for the American officers until they arrived," Joe said to me when I asked him how he had managed. Apparently, the German people were as tired of all the fighting as we were!

From May onward, it was obvious that we would soon be returning home, so we frequently found time to fit in some sightseeing and exploring.

One such time came at a break following some shows for the infantry based east of Schwerin. "Would you like to meet some Russian soldiers?" our Special Services officer inquired. Don and I agreed immediately, and Sandy, too, gave an enthusiastic OK.

After a little haggling with the guards about a mile east of the camp where we had been entertaining, we were finally allowed to proceed. Soon we were stopped by a company of Russian soldiers. Our Special Services officer explained that we were only interested in shaking hands with our Russian allies, and the icy atmosphere we had felt began to melt.

We started around the circle of soldiers, shaking hands, and greeting each other in halting Russian and English. Things were going so well, that Don decided to reach for his little Brownie camera. "Think I'll get a couple pictures," he said as he started to put some film into the camera.

"Nyet! Nyet!" The sergeant in charge made his meaning very clear. Even if we had had any doubts, they would have been promptly dispelled by the rifles and machine guns that were being aimed right at us!

When he heard the clicks of the loaded hand guns, Don suddenly discovered that he had run out of film, and that we had run out of time for visiting. We promptly got into our jeep, but Don just had to get in one parting shot, "It'll be a long time before I do a show for you guys!"

I've always felt that if only I'd had my "squeeze box," they may have better understood our intentions.

The manager of the local German opera company offered to stage a performance for the American soldiers of the area. It seemed like a good opportunity to begin more normal relations with the German civilians, so we looked

90

forward to seeing *Weiner Blut* in the Schwerin Opera House.

The audience was ominously quiet as curtain time neared; then, at five minutes before the hour, the orchestra filed in and the oboe player sounded an A to signal the beginning of their warmup. Thirty seconds before the hour, the conductor walked to the podium, acknowledged the smattering of applause, and then, precisely on the hour, gave the down-beat. (Now I often wonder if Lawrence inherited his passion for punctuality from his German ancestors.)

I was fascinated with the performance of the musicians, actors, and actresses. And by the conductor, who sat on a tall stool and directed the orchestra with a minimum of arm-waving and histrionics.

I felt the mood of the audience change as the opera progressed; music was once again dispelling the recent feelings of hatred and suspicion. The audience and cast were molded into one "family"; music had the power to do what words could not. The applause at the end of the performance was thunderous as the audience gave a standing ovation and demanded many curtain calls.

Everyone in the orchestra and cast, and most of the audience, was crying from sheer happiness and relief. Somehow we knew that these Germans were trying to tell us there would never be another Hitler; that there would never again be any death camps; and that they, too, hoped for peace and harmony.

July 2, 1945 was a very happy day—and a very sad day. Don, Phyllis, Sandy and I were driven to Paris to entrain for LeHavre where the boat would be waiting to take us home. We each embraced Barb one last time, and wished him a good trip home when his time came. Then came the time we all dreaded most—we had to say goodbye to GI Joe. He had come along on the trip to Paris, and would be sent to a resettlement camp from there. Joe and I had become so close it was like saying goodbye to a younger brother. I embraced and held him for a long time. Finally, both of us overcome with emotion, I let go of him and said, "Goodbye, Joe. God be with you!"

Joe's last word to me was, "Shalom."

I wondered as I watched Joe's small figure disappear as the train pulled away from the station, "Will I ever see Joe again?"

Only time would tell.

Going Home

"The beginning of another chapter," I mused as our train picked up speed heading westward to Le Havre. Again the rails were singing to me, but this time, "Going home, going home."

The French countryside flashed by. Peaceful now where just twelve months before there had been masses of Army transports—first German, then Allied. The scars of war were being healed by time and nature. Some peasants in the fields reminded me of *All Quiet on the Western Front*: I wondered how long it would be until these people were once again uprooted by the agony of war. Or, as we all hoped, were we at last entering into the thousand years of peace that had been promised for so long?

Similar scenes came to my mind; in Germany, Scandinavia, Russia, even the Far East, where fighting still continued, people would be starting the struggle to put their lives back in order. I prayed that the peace would indeed last forever.

I thought of all the wonderful people I had met through USO shows: entertainers, musicians, and especially the audiences. What a priceless experience! There was a sudden pang; maybe I should have gone on to Italy or to the South Pacific with the rest of my group. But I was overcome by an even stronger desire to see Berdyne, my family, and friends. (Time would prove that I had made the right choice; the airplane carrying the USO troop I would have been with crashed over New Guinea a few months later!)

The train was moving all too slowly; I was still at the beginning of a five-thousand-mile trip. (In later years I would hear my feeling echo in the voices of my five young daughters, as they chorused, "Are we there yet, Daddy? How much farther?"—sometimes before we had even left the driveway! But all these blessings were still ahead of me.)

I sat quietly, remembering the church in Heerlen where I had knelt and thanked the Lord for sparing my life that morning so many months ago. I thanked Him again now as I saw the spires of churches along the way.

"*Nous sommes arrivés à Le Havre*." The conductor's announcement that we had arrived in Le Havre broke into my reveries. A Special Services truck was waiting to take us to our last billet in Europe, Camp Home Run. I thought, "What a perfect name!"

Here we waited for five days while our ship was being loaded. Even though we kept busy doing shows every day and evening, the time seemed endless.

At last our ship was loaded and ready to leave. We were to board the *George W. Goethals* at six o'clock on the morning of July 8. My own load as we were driven to the dock was much lighter than it had been upon my arrival in Europe. This time I had no bedroll, canteen, gas mask, or knapsack, but I believe even with that extra weight, my step would have been light!

The *George W. Goethals* was not only lighter and smaller than the *Aquitania* there was one other very important difference. It was a hospital ship, and it was

94

completely loaded with wounded soldiers on their way home.

We watched as men with arms or legs missing moved awkwardly up the gangplank on crutches. Stretcher bearers maintained a constant traffic of burn cases, double amputees, and other terribly wounded survivors of the war. In spite of the massive injuries they had all suffered, I saw not one unhappy face among our special passengers. They were going home; that's all any of us talked about.

In evacuation hospitals I had seen many men with burns over ninety percent of their bodies. The medics had performed miracles with many of them. If any good had come out of the war, it had to be the new ways to treat and heal severe burns. One of the doctors in the burn ward of a Paris hospital had been from Sioux Falls; his dedication was typical of all the doctors and nurses I met while in Europe.

Our quarters were close enough to the hospital wards that we could hear the screams of the wounded as they relived the moments of their injuries in their dreams. Awake, these same men would stoically endure any amount of pain—some even joking and flirting with the nurses as their dressings were changed and wounds treated. I was particularly impressed by the courage of the burn patients; many of them had little or no skin left to protect them, and they were in constant terrible pain that no drugs could ease.

Phyllis, Don, and I walked slowly through the wards, playing, singing, or telling jokes, but mostly just visiting and getting acquainted with these brave men. We were frustrated at not being able to help them physically, but the doctors told us how important our visits were, because they helped take their minds off the pain. The old familiar songs were the most popular—giving the men happy memories from their past lives to hang onto now, when they needed all the happiness they could get. What a tremendous debt we all owe to the men and women who were inspired to write these wonderful songs. I have always felt that they had a direct link to the mind of God.

Each afternoon I would lean on the rail of the deck and watch the waves. Of course we were traveling much slower than we did on the *Aquitania*, but this time we were on a direct course—and for America. And the sea was very calm—in direct contrast to the storms we had encountered twelve months before, when we were headed toward Europe. Even the Atlantic seemed to sense that peace once again reigned in at least half the world. The gentle, rolling swells reminded me of the great wheat fields in the Midwest, where farmers would be getting ready for the harvest right about now. I was longing to see those wheat fields again.

Even today I find tranquility in the sight of the ocean. Berdyne's great interest in painting has taught me to appreciate the myriad shapes and colors of the clouds in a sunrise or sunset over the ocean. I remember Pa saying that God paints a picture in nature to remind us of His ever-present love and watchfulness.

I find the same healing peace of mind in music and prayer. I pray, "Lord, I've too many burdens to bear alone. Please help me," and He sends music to ease the load for a moment. The music can be the babbling of a brook, the chuckle of a baby, the song of a bird—it can even be the music of my accordion.

The movement of the ship, the salt air, and the ever-changing panorama of sky and sea were a potion that heightened my awareness of myself and gave me a feeling of abounding good health. I thought of my "heart problems" and realized that, in all the activity of the past year, it had never skipped a beat. "Thank you, God," I thought. "Please keep it going, because I need at least a century to do all I would like to do. But I will accept whatever time You give me and be happy. I pray for GI Joe and the millions like him, who must be shown that life still has meaning. And that there is still a place in the world where each person can follow his own star."

On our eighth day at sea, the captain announced that we would arrive in Boston harbor early the next morning. My momentary disappointment at not seeing the Statue of Liberty passed quickly, and an air of excitement began to build throughout the ship. All of us with the Camp Shows were invited to the captain's table for dinner that last night out, and the fellowship that developed remains among my fondest memories.

During the day we had toured the wards one last time, and most of our conversation was about the admiration we felt for these brave men who held such hope in the face of everything they had gone through.

As we were nudged into Boston harbor, Sandy, Don, P.J., and I stood together at the rail. Sandy suddenly spoke up: "There's Woodside Street. I'll be home fifteen minutes after we get through customs. I'll think of you all while I'm enjoying my tea."

He spoke lightly, but we all knew what was in his heart, because we were all thinking the same thing: "We're a great team. Why do we have to break up? Will I ever see these great pals again?" I felt the familiar smarting in my eyes, and noticed that as I turned to wipe away the quick tears, Sandy, P.J., and Don were having the very same problem.

The entertainment business must cause more *good-byes* than any other business. We form small groups, do a few shows together, and then find that we have to part and move on. Most of my really close friendships have been with people with whom I have worked for only very short times.... I guess you could say there are more *hellos* in this business, too!

Almost before we knew it, we were off the boat saying good-bye to Sandy. Then Don, P.J., and I grabbed a taxi to the train station so we could hurry to New York and make travel arrangements for home. While there we still had some USO business to finish up—sort of a mustering out. Then in the hotel lobby close to the station we spent a couple of hours reminiscing, exchanging addresses, and wondering if we would ever meet again. (We would. A few years later we discovered we had all ended up in the same city!) Finally wishing each other Godspeed and good luck, we parted.

I had one last bit of business in New York before going home; my "best friend" was ailing and needed a few new reeds, so I took the accordion to the factory in lower Manhattan for service.

I had phoned Berdyne from Boston, but now I called her again, telling her when I would be home. She sounded the same; I wondered if she would look the same.

As I watched the countryside of our great nation slip swiftly by from my seat in the Twentieth Century Limited, I wondered if Berdyne and my family had changed much. They no doubt were wondering the same about me. Then every once in a while, I would bring out the accordion and begin to play to pass the time. The passengers—mostly GIs—gathered around and began to sing; the time seemed to go much faster, at least it did for me.

At long last the conductor strolled through the car with the long-awaited announcement: "Next stop, Sioux Falls. Twenty minutes." He sure didn't have to remind me!

98

I had gathered up my belongings an hour earlier and placed them near the door!

Surely it couldn't take this long for twenty minutes to pass. I looked at my watch; it must have stopped! I noticed others checking their watches, too. One soldier held his up to his ear, shook it, then looked sheepishly around to see if anyone had witnessed his impatience. I laughed with him.

"We're all in the same boat," I said to him. "How long have you been gone?"

"Four years," he stammered. "It sure will be good to get home!"

"What branch of service were you in?" I asked.

"Well," he replied, "I've been in the Air Force, but I spent the last four years in a German POW camp. I noticed your USO patch; my wife was in the USO, too."

"Did she by any chance sing "How Deep Is the Ocean?'" I asked.

"I'm sure she did," he said. "It's her favorite song. How did you know?"

"You'll never believe this," I answered him, "but I heard her sing it a year ago on the ship that took me to Europe."

"Isn't it a small world?" we both said together. Then we looked out the window and realized that the train had stopped at the Sioux Falls station at last.

"There she is!!" he shouted, drowning out my own exclamation. "There they are!"

"God bless you," he said. "And you," I replied. We were home at last.

August 19, 1945

There they were: Berdyne, Ma and Pa, my sisters and brothers...everyone had come to meet me, and we were all talking, laughing, and crying at once. I hugged Ma, and she murmured, "Thank God you're home at last!" Pa stood by quietly with big tears running down his face. I turned to him, and he said, "I knew you'd be back safe and sound, because I prayed so hard!"

A redcap lifted my accordion and suitcases down from the train and waved away the fifty-cent tip I offered. "It's good to see you back, Myron," he laughed. "Now, just keep that music coming!"

"I will," I assured him. "I sure will!"

We drove to my folks' little house, where Ma had prepared a special supper of *lefse* and baked Spam. (I didn't have the heart to tell her that after a year of K rations, in which *Spam* was usually the main course, I could barely stand the *sight* of it—much less the taste!) The *lefse* was the very best I had ever tasted!

How good it was to hear familiar voices and see those loving faces again. I thanked the Lord several times that evening as cousins, aunts, uncles, even some new brothers-in-law came by to say hello. We talked and visited all evening until finally Berdyne, who had stood quietly beside me during all the commotion, tugged on my sleeve and asked, "Could you take me home, now, please?"

When we got in the car, I asked, "Are you in a hurry to get home?"

"Not especially," she answered. "No, I'm in no hurry."

"Let's drive around for a while then," I suggested. We drove to one of our favorite spots south of Sioux Falls, where we could sit in the car and watch the lights.

"Do you still want to get married?" I asked.

"Yes," she replied. "If you do."

"I sure do!" I said. "How about tomorrow?" I was so glad to see her, I doubted that I could wait much longer!

"Not that fast," she laughed. "We need a little time to get to know each other again. It's been so long. Besides, I need time to plan the wedding, get out invitations, arrange for someone to sing and play the organ...so many things. How about August 19?"

"Sounds great to me. August 19 it is!"

My schedule began to fill up almost immediately with interviews, appearances, wedding plans, visits with old friends...then the whole world stood still at the headlines on August 6: "ATOM BOMB DEVASTATES HIRO-SHIMA!" Our local paper, *The Argus Leader,* went on to describe the awesome destruction that the world's first atomic bomb had caused in the Japanese city. The Japanese commanders were meeting in special session; panic was beginning to spread over all of Japan. I believe that we were all too stunned by the magnitude of the weapon to realize it could mean a quick end to the war.

Then, just three days later, the headlines again jumped out at us: "SECOND ATOM BOMB STRIKES NAGASAKI." This time we all knew...the war would soon be finished. On August 14 the Japanese War Council decided to accept the Allied peace settlement, and the emperor capitulated on the following day. We heard that his speech of surrender was the first time the Japanese people had ever heard the voice of their leader!

The long, long war was over at last; people were dancing in the streets! A nationwide celebration began and lasted for days. How wonderful that we could start our marriage without the threat of war hanging over our heads!

Our plans for August 19 went on without a hitch. Gas rationing was lifted; there were no more food-rationing stamps; shortages of all kinds began to disappear. President Truman led the nation in prayers of thanksgiving. Thousands of lives had been destroyed by the atomic bombs, but who knew how many more thousands might have been lost if the war had been allowed to continue.

So on August 19, Berdyne and I and our families were not the only people with reason to celebrate; it seemed like the whole world was in a party mood.

Reverend Glenn performed the ceremony in the First Lutheran Church of Sioux Falls; it's a place we still like to visit on our trips back home today. Our friend Betty Brumbaugh sang "O Promise Me" and "*Jeg Elsker Deg*" ("I Love You"), the latter a favorite Norwegian wedding song. The church was full to overflowing with relatives, friends...and *fans!* After the ceremony, everyone gathered in the reception hall for cake and coffee. We were both a little overwhelmed by the hundreds of people who had come to share our day.

Berdyne's parents, Ed and Albena Koerner, had invited all the relatives to their house after the reception to enjoy a light supper and watch us open our gifts. About eleven that evening, we slipped away for the hour-long drive to Pipestone, Minnesota, where we planned to spend our first night as Mr. and Mrs. To tell the truth, most of our wedding day is a big blur to me now, but I'll never forget how beautiful Berdyne looked as she walked down the aisle on her father's arm!

During the drive to Pipestone, Berdyne asked me to please *not* mention the fact that we had just been married. I agreed that it would be too embarrassing and assured her as we pulled to a stop in front of the hotel that I wouldn't do such a silly thing.

"You know, we just got married!" I heard myself say to the desk clerk as I signed the register. (I know; I can't believe it either!)

"Congratulations," the clerk answered, cleverly concealing his enthusiasm with a huge yawn. "Here's your key." Glancing at the clock, which read 12:30 A.M., he asked, "Need any help with your luggage? No, I see you can handle it. Good night, folks."

I couldn't understand why Berdyne's face was such a bright shade of red as we walked to our room!

We had reservations at Hultgren's Lodge on Green Lake in Minnesota and got up early the next morning for the remainder of our honeymoon drive. We checked into the lodge a little after noon, and this time I managed not to mention our recent wedding. I was feeling very pleased with myself, when I heard a loud voice from across the room: "Myron Floren! What are you doing here? Oh, that's right, you just got married; I was at the wedding! Congratulations! This must be the blushing bride!"

Well, he was right about *that*; I've never seen anyone turn *so many* shades of red...and still look so lovely! About forty pairs of eyes turned toward us. Seeing the stir he had created, my friend said, "Gee, I'm sorry; I didn't mean to let the cat out of the bag!"

"Oh, that's all right," I said to him, remembering Pa's advice about spilled milk. "They'd have found out sooner or later, anyway."

104

The desk clerk handed me the key to our room and said, "Your honeymoon suite is down by the lake. Would you like some help with your bags?"

"No," I answered. "We just have a couple small bags and my accordion. I can handle it."

At the word "accordion" those forty eyes were on us again. I could just hear those people thinking, "Accordion?!"

Now it was my turn to blush! "Well," I said, "I thought I might want to practice in my spare time." Again, I felt the thoughts..."Practice!"..."Spare time??!"

We got out of there fast then and headed for our "honeymoon suite." Just as the clerk had said, it was right on the lake; and from the outside, it looked nice and roomy.

I said to Berdyne as I unlocked the door, "Wait till you see this nice room!" I opened the door and we walked in together. I placed the suitcases on the floor and put the accordion in the closet with a silent promise to myself that it would *stay* there till we were ready to leave!

When I turned to Berdyne to give her a big hug, I noticed that she was standing very still, looking at the wall above the bed. I followed her gaze and discovered that there was an open space about a foot down from the ceiling the whole length of the room. We were in a duplex, and the wall separating us from the apartment next door was open at the top!

"Oh no!" Berdyne said, as she sat down on the bed. I felt the walls begin to close in on me—that had to be the squeakiest bed I had ever heard! And I'd heard a lot of them!

"Honey," I said, "let's go have some supper. Maybe we can get another room; I'll check with the desk clerk while we're down there."

"Okay," she said. "Maybe we could just get something

with a little more privacy?"

I stopped by the desk and was assured that by the next day we would be moved to another room. We went into the dining room and found a fairly private table where, I thought, we could enjoy each other's company for a little while before we headed back to our "semi-private room." As we finished our dinner, my friend came by with some of the other guests to wish us well. We thanked them, and said good night to all our new friends.

Back in our room, I gave Berdyne a big hug, and we decided to forget about the hole in the wall for one night. Then she said, "Why don't you get comfortable. I'm going to take a bath."

She turned and walked to the bathroom door, only to find it locked from the inside. We were sharing the bathroom with the other room also!

As we stood together in front of the bathroom door—under the hole in the wall—trying to decide whether to laugh or cry, we heard a loud knock on the door.

It was my friend with the big mouth again! "We thought you might be feeling lonesome. There are about fifty of us relaxing down in the lobby. We were wondering if you might come down and play for us."

Berdyne sighed and shrugged. "We might as well go on down there," she said. "I think this evening has had it anyway."

I must admit that I was a big hit that evening...and the next seven evenings as well. When we were ready to leave, the hotel guests gave us a lovely silver cream-and-sugar set as a thank-you for entertaining them. We never did get a private room, but things did improve later in the week when our neighbors in the duplex checked out, leaving the whole cottage all to us.

You know, from that honeymoon on, I've always had trouble getting Berdyne to come along on trips with me. I can't figure out where I might have gone wrong!

The Joe Howard Show

When we returned from our honeymoon, Berdyne and I set up housekeeping in a three-room apartment owned by a friend of hers. We were lucky to get it; housing after the war was tight. My cup was running over. Our time together could only be called blissful, and my work was more in demand than ever. I had resumed my broadcasts over KSOO; they consisted of two solo programs every day along with guest appearances with various country and old-time groups. I was having a great time and making a better living than I ever thought possible.

My family was still living in the same house we had rented before the war. Pa had found a building lot that he could get by paying about two hundred dollars in back taxes. The folks asked if I would help them. I had saved about five thousand dollars and the idea of building a house interested me. All of the family pitched in to help build the house. I had a lot of fun helping dig the basement and doing some of the carpentry work. Pa had never had any formal training in construction but he had a practical mind for putting things together.

The work came along rapidly, and it looked as if the house would be finished before cold weather set in. By the time of the September Sioux Empire Fair, we were already closing in the framework and shingling the roof. I put in all the time I could in between my radio shows and other appearances.

I was just leaving our apartment one Saturday morning to work on the house when the phone rang. It was the secretary at KSOO.

"We've just had a call from the fairgrounds," she said. "Joe Howard's accordion player is sick, and we told him you'd be just the one to help out. Rehearsal is in one hour— at ten o'clock. Can you be there?"

"Sure," I said. "I'll go right out."

"Honey," I hung up the phone and turned to Berdyne, "the fair board wants me to go out to the fair and play for Joe Howard!"

"Who's Joe Howard?" she asked.

"He's a famous entertainer," I answered, "and he's written a lot of songs, like 'I Wonder Who's Kissing Her Now' and 'School Days.' Want to come along?"

"I'd like to," she said, "but I promised the folks I'd visit them today. Maybe we'll come out later to hear your show."

I arrived at the fairgrounds a few minutes before ten and went right into the tent for rehearsal. I was the first person there, so I got out my accordion to practice for a few minutes. Right at ten, in walked this little old man—kind of like Santa Claus without a beard. His cherubic, happy face put me at ease before he even uttered a word. He came right over and shook hands, saying, "Hello, I'm Joe Howard. You must be the accordion player that the radio station sent over."

I assured him that I was and added, "Mr. Howard, I've played all of your songs on my radio programs." Well! I could tell that put me on third base already!

110

We started going through his act, and I had no problem with any of the music. "Would you do a couple of numbers on the show?" he asked.

(Would I?!) "I'd love to," I answered nonchalantly. "I have a lot of relatives coming to the show, and they'd like that."

We were set to do both an afternoon and an evening show that day. The matinee went fine, and I got a big hand for my solos *and* my accompaniment. After the show, Mr. Howard asked if he could talk to me a bit. We went back into the tent, and he told me to sit down and listen.

"I think you are wasting your time here. You should try for something on a national level. If you'd like, I'll call my agent in Chicago and have him look around. It may take a little while, but he'll find something. I predict you'll go to the top!"

I wasn't prepared for *this*!

"Mr. Howard," I said, "you've kind of taken my breath away with your advice. I need to think about all this and talk it over with my wife. I'll let you know before the second show."

"Okay," he answered. "But I've never been more serious. And don't forget you're just the right age to try for the top of this business. If you wait too long, you'll get too settled here, and it will be too hard to leave."

"I'll let you know tonight, Mr. Howard. I promise."

Berdyne had supper ready when I reached home between shows. "Honey," I said rather tentatively, "Joe Howard thinks I should try for something bigger in music than I could ever hope to have here in Sioux Falls. He wants me to have his agent, Bill Ellsworth in Chicago, try to find me something. It will mean leaving our home and friends here, and it could mean a lot of time apart, but I feel I should try to go as high as I can in music. Maybe in the future we can have something really worthwhile. Music is a big part of everyone's life, and if I could become well known, I think I could do a lot of good things."

At first she just sat quietly, thinking, then: "I would miss my friends and family here, but if you think you really want this, I'll go with you, and I'm sure we can be happy. We'll make a good home wherever we go. I knew when I married you that your heart was in music. As long as I'm with you, I know that I'll be happy."

Berdyne's eyes were shining when she finished that long speech, but I knew she meant all she said and that we would be following our own star wherever it would lead.

After the evening show, I approached Mr. Howard.

"Well, did you decide to take my advice?" he asked.

"Yes, Mr. Howard," I replied. "Berdyne and I talked it all over, and we're ready to go anywhere we're called."

"I'm happy to hear it," he said, shaking my hand warmly. "I know that you won't be sorry. By the way, I went ahead and called my agent this afternoon, and he's already looking around. You'll be hearing from him soon. Good luck to you both; may God be with you."

On Monday morning I started to tell a few people about my decision. Sioux Falls had never looked more beautiful to me. Leaves were turning red and gold with the bite of an early frost, and the air tasted fresh as new snow.

My first stop was KSOO, where I found Mort Hankin seated at the piano improvising a cute arrangement of "After You've Gone." "Coincidence?" I wondered, or had he guessed what I was going to say by noting the expression on my face?

As I walked in, his eyes lit up, and he said, "Hi, Myron. Sit down. Joe Howard called me this morning before he left town and told me what a fine job you did for him at the

112

fair. He also told me what he advised you to do. I think I would try if I were you. We'll miss you, but we would never be able to pay you what you can earn by going national. Just remember, though, if things don't work out like you want them to, you're always welcome back here!"

I thanked him and added, "You've made this first step almost painless. Telling my family won't be so easy."

I picked Berdyne up at the apartment, and we drove to Pa's half-finished house. After the usual greetings, I got serious. "Pa and Ma, you know I played for Joe Howard at the fair this past week...and he thinks I should move on to some bigger opportunities in music. He's having his agent in Chicago look for something for me right now. I told him I was ready anytime he called."

There. Everything was out in the open. My folks looked at each other for a long time before speaking. Finally Ma said, "I'll go make some coffee. I baked cinnamon rolls this morning. Berdyne, would you like to help me?"

Pa and I were left alone. He slowly stood up and walked to the table to pick up his can of Prince Albert tobacco. He had a hard time getting the tobacco to stay on the paper as he tried to roll a cigarette. I could see he was wrestling with his emotions. Finally he lit the cigarette and took a puff. Blowing the smoke out into the chilly fall air, he said, "Yes, I've known for a long time that you would have to leave here eventually. Sioux Falls just doesn't have enough opportunity for your career to grow. You know that we'll miss you. And we know you'll never forget the people that really love you."

Knowing how hard it was for Pa to see any of us leave, I assured them that distance would never cause me to forget the wonderful years back on the farm. We would miss the family as much as they would miss us. I would be forever grateful for the love they had shown me as I grew up. "Besides," I reminded them, "we aren't leaving tomorrow. That agent probably won't find anything for me for quite a while."

"Don't worry," Pa answered. "I think it will be sooner than you expect. Now, let's go have a cinnamon roll and some coffee."

In the kitchen, we all talked at once as we tried to guess where we might end up. I helped as Pa finished nailing up the siding, and as we worked I wondered just what the future might bring. Whatever it was, I was confident that it would be right. I could feel God's hands guiding me once again, just as He had during my attacks of rheumatic fever and all during my travels in Europe. I knew all I was required to do was let Those hands lead me where I should go.

The Buckeye Four
and St. Louis

The next few weeks passed quickly. We celebrated Thanksgiving in my parents' newly completed house and Christmas with Berdyne's parents and her sister, Betty.

Shortly after New Year's Day 1946, I came home from my noon program on KSOO and Berdyne handed me a telegram. It was unopened. "Why didn't you open it?" I asked.

"It was addressed to you. And besides, I don't like telegrams. I'm afraid it might be bad news."

I opened it quickly and read, "Can you join Buckeye Four—KWK Radio and Mutual Network, St. Louis... March 15. Please advise... Bill Ellsworth."

"Honey," I said, "it's what we've been waiting for. It's an offer of a job with the Buckeye Four in St. Louis. They want me to report by March 15."

We spent the next eight weeks winding up our business in Sioux Falls—saying a lot of good-byes and accepting wishes for good luck and happiness. Luckily we had not yet accumulated any bulky or hard-to-handle items, and our 1938 Lafayette easily held the few things we would take with us at first.

115

We drove to St. Louis and checked into the Forest Park Hotel. The Shady Valley Folks, of which the Buckeye Four was a major part, did their mutual broadcast every morning from KWK in the Chase Hotel—only a couple of blocks away. That first evening in St. Louis was very lonesome for Berdyne and me. We sat together in our room wondering if we had done the right thing, leaving our families and familiar surroundings in Sioux Falls for this huge, strange city.

Our doubts were dispelled the next day when we met my new employers for the first time. We knew right away that we would all become fast friends. The Buckeye Four consisted of "Horseshoe Mike" Riaff on violin; "Cowboy Joe" Randall, guitar and vocal; Si Wilkins, bass and comedy vocal; and now I would fill the fourth spot. The Shady Valley Folks' emcee was Jack Dunnigan, who also sang duets with his wife, Gertrude. The other members were Tommy and Mary Lou Sutton, also vocalists. Their show was heard all over the country on the Mutual Radio Network. I could feel the pattern of our future being forged.

In just a few days, I was settled into my new routine. Berdyne and I spent our afternoons looking for an apartment. Our situation was rather common: a young married couple with no children, no pets, no furniture, and no bank balance. Finally I noticed an ad in the *St. Louis Post Dispatch*: "Sleeping room with kitchen privileges in Richmond Heights." I called the telephone number in the ad and found that the room was still available. "We'll take it!" I said. Then I thought, "Maybe we'd better go see it before we decide for sure."

The drive to Richmond Heights was only about twenty minutes, an acceptable distance. We found the house on a quiet residential street; the idea of renting just a room became a little more appealing. I rang the bell and

116

immediately liked the young couple who answered the door. They were about our age and seemed like nice people. They also had a cute little baby boy. The room was charming, so we decided to move in as their first renters. Their names were John and Gladys Watts. I was very pleased; everything seemed to be falling right into place. After only one week in St. Louis, in addition to a good job, we already had a home, and some new friends.

(The Watts' had a TV set in their living room. Up until then, TV was something we had only heard about, and we soon became avid watchers in our spare time. Our particular favorites were Milton Berle and the wrestling matches. I don't really remember if there was much of anything else on at the time.)

I enjoyed my work with the Buckeye Four. We became close friends as well as partners in business. One or the other of us was always having a party. The most popular get-togethers were backyard barbecues—something new to Berdyne and me. Potato salad and hot dogs were almost always served as the main course, and to this day they always signal a party to me! We discovered new friends and neighbors every week. Some of them are still close to us today.

Two of our particularly close friends were Ace and Alfreda Nash. Ace was an accordionist with much the same ambitions as mine. Berdyne and Alfreda became fast friends almost upon their first meeting. Ace and Alfreda had been married longer than we had, and they had two little girls that we fell in love with.

My radio work didn't take up all my time, so I practiced a lot and even tried my hand at writing a few original melodies. I submitted all my music to the Alfred Music Company in New York. Mr. Sam Manus, the owner of the company, finally accepted some for publication: "Dakota

Polka," "Windy River," and the "Florena Polka."

I had heard of the big money earned by songwriters and looked forward eagerly to my first royalty check. We were using some of my music on the Shady Valley shows, so I figured my first check would be a whopper!

A few months into 1948, my first check arrived. Berdyne and I looked at the envelope for a long time before we opened it. We discussed where we should invest it. She thought maybe a home of our own ... then decided it might not be *that* much and suggested a "big" ten-inch television set, some new clothes, or a nice vacation trip. Finally after a few cups of coffee, I picked up the envelope and read the amount.

"Honey, how about hamburgers for two at the White Castle for starters and then maybe a movie. The check is for twenty-seven dollars and four cents."

We both laughed, and Berdyne added, "Maybe it's just as well. Anything that easy to come by just isn't worthwhile."

And that's been part of my philosophy ever since. As my friend Tom Purdum from New Braunfels, Texas, says, "Expect nothing; then anything that comes along will seem like a nice surprise." Or, as Lawrence Welk once said, "Don't count your chickens till they cross the street!"

After about a year in St. Louis, I felt that my name was becoming pretty well known. And sure enough, one Saturday evening I got a call from the Busch family to come play at a little family gathering in their home. Two problems loomed, though, that almost stopped me from taking the job. The St. Louis musicians union had allowed the Buckeye Four to play in their jurisdiction without transferring their union cards. That meant that no member of the quartet could work solo in the St. Louis area. My understanding with Horseshoe Mike and Cowboy Joe was that I would

118

play only with them. But we had agreed on that only to avoid breaking any union rules. In Sioux Falls, of course, I had always belonged to the musicians' union, and the officials had all been friends of mine. From what I had heard of Mr. James C. Petrillo and the strong union around the country, I wasn't about to go against any of their rules.

I was in a real quandary. I couldn't reach anybody by phone: both Mike and Joe were out of town with their families and Local 2 of the American Federation of Musicians was closed for the weekend.

. While I was trying to locate someone from the group or union, a representative of the Busch family called back to beg me to come. "Look, we'll pay you fifty dollars!" Now, even I knew *that* was way over scale!

"Well, OK," I said haltingly. "I guess if you're in a spot, I could help you out and then square it with the union on Monday."

"Don't worry about the union," the caller said. "We know them well, and if there's any problem, we'll help you out."

That settled it. A little while later, I arrived at the Busch home with my accordion in hand. Someone told me to just stroll around while I played, so I was able to get a really good look at this mansion, which reminded me some of the huge estates I had lived in with the USO in Germany. I wanted to remember every detail to tell Berdyne later.

The party started off rather sedately, but as the evening progressed, the requests changed from semi-classical music to good old sing-along type melodies in both German and English. I learned some songs that evening that I still use today.

Well, Monday morning arrived all too fast. I told the other members what had happened over the weekend and stressed the fact that I had tried to reach them. The silence was deafening, broken finally by the KWK operator calling to tell Mike that there was a call for him from the musicians' union. Mike looked at me accusingly. "Now we're in for it!" he said.

He walked out to the phone; in a couple of minutes, he returned—all smiles!

"That was the local secretary," he said happily. "Mr. Busch *himself* called them this morning to explain about the weekend, and they'd like us to join the union as full-fledged members. We lucked out, but I sure was spinning there for a minute!"

My relations with the Local 2 in St. Louis were always very cordial, and to this day I keep my card paid up!

Berdyne and I were beginning to feel a little cramped in our rented room and decided to start looking for something a little larger. One day we visited Jack and Gertrude Dunnigan in their little twenty-seven-foot trailer house in Overland, a suburb of St. Louis. The trailer looked so comfortable there under the giant oak trees that I impulsively said, "Jack, if you ever want to sell this, please let us have first chance on it."

"As a matter of fact, Gertrude and I are leaving for New York State soon, so the trailer is already for sale!" Jack answered.

That's how we happened to become two of the first "trailerites" in the country back in 1948! I built a nice porch on the front of our new "home" and Berdyne added a mailbox with our name on it. We were so tickled with that little place—we felt like real property owners! Mr. Dees, who owned the tavern on the corner nearest us, also owned the land the trailer was parked on, so we paid him rent every month. We had to walk about fifty paces to our private

120

bathroom in the basement of the tavern. Except in winter, it was very handy.

I put in running water and a fifty-gallon fuel tank for the stove. Sometimes water would get into the kerosene, and I'd have a hard time unfreezing the fuel lines. Another little problem was caused by acorns and branches that fell on the canvas roof of the trailer during storms. Sometimes I had to patch hundreds of leaky little holes in our roof!

Berdyne and I had been married about four years by this time, and of course the in-laws on both sides were campaigning for grandchildren. Traditionally, the first child arrived near the end of the first year of marriage, and when that hadn't happened with us, we became the butt of a lot of silly jokes. We had decided to wait till my career became a bit more settled and money a little more sure. The Buckeye Four was beginning to do a lot of traveling, and Berdyne was often alone for days while we did jobs in Illinois, Ohio, and even as far away as Pennsylvania. At last we realized that things would probably never be settled in the usual sense of the word, so we made plans to start our family. We decided that we would convert the bedroom of our little trailer into a room for the baby when the time came, and we would sleep on the sofa. Cramped quarters, to be sure, but *so* cozy!

It was about this same time, too, that I contacted the Ludwig Music Store in St. Louis. They were making a big business out of teaching veterans on the GI Bill and needed an accordion teacher, since the accordion was becoming a big favorite with many of the ex-soldiers. Eventually I wound up with about ninety students a week.

My schedule was full to overflowing when the Shady Valley Folks decided to enter into a contract with KSD-TV to appear on a weekly musical program. I was seeing so little of Berdyne that it began to seem as if our family plans

121

would be indefinitely postponed! At last we found Charlie Ackerman, a singer reminiscent of the style of Arthur Godfrey, to take Jack Dunnigan's place. That gave me a little free time, since Charlie took over some of the duties I had inherited from Jack.

Between teaching, practicing, radio, television, and personal appearances, our trailer had become my island of peace. Financially, our lives were becoming a little easier; I counted the time payments one day and was surprised to see that money was going out on ten separate contracts. We were beginning to build a fine credit rating!

The 1949 baseball season found the Buckeye Four entertaining at many of the St. Louis Cardinal home games. I loved baseball, and playing for those games was just like an afternoon off. Every time we played "Wabash Cannon Ball," Dizzy Dean would stick his head out of the broadcast booth and wave. I still remember the day Babe Ruth made his final appearance at the ball park; he looked so thin and frail from his battle with cancer.

I came home from a baseball game one afternoon to discover Berdyne trying on a kind of wraparound dress that Alfreda had brought over. As I came through the door, I overheard her say to Berdyne, "This one will be good for many months because it can be adjusted."

"Why should it have to be adjusted?" I asked. Sometimes I'm not the most perceptive husband!

"Well, she'll be getting bigger for a while now, you know," Alfreda answered for Berdyne.

Then it hit me; I remembered a book titled *Your First Baby*—I had seen it on the kitchen table. "Honey!" I said. "You're going to have a baby!"

"You guessed," Berdyne said to me. "You've been so busy that I kind of thought I'd surprise you with a baby for your birthday in November. The baby's due in October."

122

Randee Lee joined Berdyne and me on October 13th. My cup was brimming over.

The Lawrence
Welk Show

To celebrate her birthday on March 7, 1950, Berdyne and I decided to go dancing. We went to the Casa Loma Ballroom on St. Louis's south side, where Lawrence Welk was appearing with his Champagne Music Makers.

I felt a close kinship with Mr. Welk. He was from North Dakota and I was from South Dakota. We had both been born on the farm. Our early years were similar. Working on the farm but dreaming of music. We had met casually in Sioux Falls when I worked for radio station KSOO. Berdyne and I had attended one of his dances at the Arkota Ballroom in Sioux Falls. Meg Hanson, my good friend who managed the Arkota, had introduced us. As I turned these things over in my mind, I felt that Lawrence Welk and I were already old friends.

A familiar mark of a Lawrence Welk appearance has always been a full house, and that evening was no exception. The evening was more than half over before Mr. Welk noticed me dancing with Berdyne near the stage. Soon he asked me to come up on stage and play his accordion. I chose "Lady of Spain" as a show number for the audience that had gathered to see the "special performance." I was surprised (and a little embarrassed) by the loud applause and laughter that erupted from the audience as I finished; I turned around and discovered that Mr. Welk was crouching under the piano waving a large white handkerchief in a comic sign of surrender! He has always been a great showman...and his audiences are always happy to be his "second bananas."

Then Mr. Welk brought out one of his new arrangements, a medley made up of "Million Dollar Baby," "Pretty Baby," and "Yes, Sir, That's My Baby." I glanced at the music for a few minutes and saw that the notes were fairly simple. Mr. Welk counted off the band, "Ah-one, and ah-two, and ah—" and lo and behold, I was playing with the Welk band for the first time.

I finished the medley with a flourish and handed the accordion back to Mr. Welk, who uttered a phrase then that I have heard him say many times since: "I just hate it when somebody comes up from the audience and plays better than I do!"

I started to leave the stage, and before I could get half-way down the stairs, Mr. Welk had stopped me to say, "Wait! You're not finished yet! Our Champagne Lady just told me that she would give her right arm to dance with you!"

Well, that seemed like a rather high price to pay, so I returned to the stage and the band swung into "Josephine" as I began to dance with Lawrence's Champagne Lady, Helen Ramsey. Luckily for Helen (I'm not the world's greatest dancer!) the stage was small and intermission near, so her poor feet were fairly safe!

When intermission arrived, Berdyne and I headed back toward our table. As we were sitting down, I noticed that Mr. Welk had followed us.

126

"May I join you?" he asked as he pulled a chair up to the table. Then: "How would you like to join our band?" (He doesn't beat around the bush. It's a trait that sometimes seems a little abrupt, but cuts away a lot of meaningless talk and gets right to the heart of the subject.)

While I was collecting my thoughts enough to be able to speak, he continued to Berdyne, "Mrs. Floren, I think your husband has what it takes to make it right to the top in this business, and I'd like to help him. We have a show on the ABC radio network for a national sponsor. We would feature him on that and on our personal-appearance tours where we play a different city each night."

Then to me: "I'm getting too busy with the management of the band. I don't have time to practice anymore. Do you like to practice?"

I assured him that I did! And he answered, "Well, then, how about it?"

Then, as now, Mr. Welk could be very persuasive. So far, I had only read about the traveling bands and their "one-nighters," but the idea of playing and practicing every day really appealed to me. We would have to sell our little trailer, of course, but that would be no problem. Randee, not yet a year old, and Berdyne would have to put up with a lot of discomfort on the road ... so would I, for that matter. Then I thought of my students at Ludwig's; they still had three months left on their semester for the GI Bill.

At last I emerged from my fog of excitement enough to notice that Berdyne was suffering conflicting emotions. She finally nodded, and I said, "Okay, Mr. Welk. What if I finish the semester at Ludwig's and then join you in June."

"That sounds fine," he answered. "Except that I think you should do some recordings with us in the meantime, and also some of our radio shows. It would mean a few trips to New York, Chicago, Rock Island, and a few other places."

I felt Berdyne squeeze my hand. Whether she did that for encouragement or from suddenly realizing the many times when we would have to be apart, I don't know. I looked at her. With her eyes shining, she finally said, "If it's what you want, then it's also what I want. Randee is too young to realize what's going on. She'll be fine as long as one of us is around."

When we returned home late that night, Berdyne checked on Randee, seven months old, sound asleep in her crib. Then we sat down together on the sofa. Neither of us spoke for a few moments. Then I started thinking out loud: "I wonder if we are doing the right thing. The events of the past three hours are going to cause a major change in our lives. We've made a lot of new friends here in St. Louis and have been able to save some money for the first time. I like the Buckeye Four and my teaching schedule at Ludwig's. And I have a feeling that my heavy schedule is going to get even heavier if I join the Welk group, but somehow I feel like it's the next step for me. My music sales will pick up when I start playing the songs on the Welk show ... that'll mean many more days on the road. It will all be pretty exciting for me, but very lonely for you. What do you really think we should do?"

"Myron, I know you well enough by now to know that you'll make the right decisions for all of us," Berdyne said. "As long as we can be together some of the time, whatever you decide will be OK."

We talked until sunrise, and when daylight began to shine through the windows, we walked out onto the little porch, where we could enjoy the freshness of the early morning. (Actually the air was a bit too fresh at about

128

thirty degrees, but we were too excited by our future to be uncomfortable at the time!) We had made up our minds; we would join Lawrence Welk on June 7, just ninety days away, at Elitch's Gardens in Denver, Colorado.

I called my folks in Sioux Falls to tell them the good news. Pa was happy for me, and very excited. Ma's reaction was a little more subdued. She thought right away about the long hours and miles of traveling that the new job would entail, and began to worry right then. I tried to reassure her, saying, "Maybe I'll be able to give my family something better in the future than we could ever afford in St. Louis."

Now I had to face telling the Buckeye Four about my plans. The next night we had a club engagement in East St. Louis; after the third set I finally got up the nerve to talk to them. They just listened quietly, until at last Horseshoe Mike extended his hand and said, "We're going to miss you, but if you feel this is what you want to do, then we wish you the best. I know you'll be a success!"

The next few weeks flew by. Besides my work at Ludwig's, the last few dates with the Buckeye Four, and the TV shows on KSD-TV, I was now busy with Lawrence Welk dates also. I made a few trips to New York to do the network radio shows for Mr. Welk and also to record a couple of records for him. We made "Dakota Polka" and "Windy River Polka" at this time. The band arrangements for those records were done by Lew Davies—a highly respected music man in New York. While in New York on one of those trips, Mr. Welk introduced me to Frances Margliss, a very outgoing young lady who was the sales manager for the firm of Ernest Deffner, Inc., which in turn handled the Pancordion made by the Crucianelli factory in Castel-

129

fidardo, Italy. I found out years later that Lawrence had relied on her opinion of my playing when he decided whether or not he would keep me with the band.

I changed to the Pancordion so that the company would be able to publicize our appearances. They took a lot of pictures to use in their advertising campaigns—I felt that I had finally joined the big time.

On my first visit to New York to work with Mr. Welk, he arranged for me to stay at the Roosevelt Hotel. While there, we met Sam Lutz, Mr. Welk's personal manager, for breakfast. He made no secret of the fact that he was very opposed to my joining the band.

"What would people say if Tommy Dorsey hired a trombone player who played better than he did?" Mr. Lutz said to Mr. Welk.

I will forever love Lawrence for his answer: "Sam, you know that's the only kind of musician I will hire for my band!"

I finally told Mr. Lutz, "Just let me try it for a year. If it doesn't work out, I can always go back to St. Louis."

On the fifth of June Berdyne and I packed all our belongings into our 1948 DeSoto and headed for Colorado. As we left St. Louis behind, Randee, sitting in her car seat between Berdyne and me, said, "Where going?"

Berdyne answered her for both of us: "We don't really know, but we're going together!"

We arrived in Denver on June 6, the day before I was to report to Mr. Welk. His motel was on the west side of Denver, on Colfax Avenue. We got settled in our room, and then advised Mr. Welk that we had arrived. His wife, Fern, and their children, Shirley, Donna, and Lawrence Welk, Jr.

(Larry), were with him on this trip, since he was to be in Denver for a couple of weeks.

The next day, at Elitch's Gardens, I officially started my career with Lawrence Welk and his Champagne Music Makers. My solo on our radio show that evening was "Lady of Spain." He arranged several times during the evening for me to "show my stuff" so he could check the audience's reactions.

During the evening I noticed a couple of people standing near the stage watching me very closely. From time to time, Mr. Welk would go over and say a few words to them, and they would again look in my direction. Finally, Mr. Welk introduced the couple—Joe and Kathryn Weitzel from Broken Bow, Nebraska—to me. He had known them for many years and wanted their opinion of my talents. Luckily for me, they enjoyed my music, and we remain the best of friends even today.

The two weeks in Denver helped Berdyne and me become used to our new way of life. We soon discovered that a group of people that works, plays, eats, lives, and argues together is just like a family. I learned that the best way to get along with everyone was to just do my job, keep my mouth shut, and listen to all the advice that was offered to me as the rookie in residence.

Mr. Welk was not in the habit of talking over his plans with members of the band. My appearance on the scene seemed especially difficult for the organist, Jerry Burke. For some reason, Jerry was convinced that I had been hired to replace *him*! One evening in Lake Geneva, Wisconsin, his uneasy feelings came out in the open. We were all sitting around visiting when Jerry suddenly became very argumentative. Everyone in the band listened for a while, and finally, the first trumpet man, Harry Gosling, spoke up: "Jerry, Myron's not here to replace you. He works hard, and we all think he's a good addition to the band, so lay off!"

Jerry and I hit it off fine after that.

My work schedule in St. Louis had been very light compared to what I had thrust myself into now. From June 7, 1950, through mid-May, 1951, we played about two hundred one-nighters all across the United States. Occasionally we would get to stay in one place for a week or so at a time...these welcome "stands" were like a vacation and gave us a chance to get our laundry done. I was earning twenty dollars a night and had to pay for motels, food, traveling expenses, and laundry out of my salary. Much of the time Berdyne and Randee traveled with me, and some weeks when we worked only three or four nights we had to watch every penny. At least we were able to find motel rooms for two to four dollars a night.

All of us were in the same boat financially and we worked many angles to save money. For example, we'd play a dance in the evening and then immediately jump in our cars and head for the next town, planning to arrive in our next destination around seven in the morning. The hotels almost all had a "day-sheet" policy, that is, if you checked in after 7 A.M., you could sleep all day, do the job that evening, then sleep again...all for the price of one night's lodging.

When Berdyne and Randee weren't with me, I rode with Lawrence and his secretary, Lois Lamont. Lawrence was very organized and dedicated. I could sense in him a quality of persistence that I have seen in very few other men. He would dictate letters while we were riding, and when we arrived at our destinations, Lois would type them up and mail them. As we prepared to enter new towns,

Lawrence would check a list of any old friends he might have in the area, so that names and families would be fresh in his memory when he greeted them.

Lawrence Welk's frugality has become something of a legend, and it all stems from his training back on the farm, where money came very hard. I remember stopping at a motel about six o'clock one morning. I got out of the car, woke the owner, and asked the room rate. He said four dollars. That sounded good to me, so I then asked him if that would include two "sleepers" (a day and a night). When I informed Lawrence that the owner wanted eight dollars per room for the two sleep periods, he shook his head and said, "No, I can't afford that. Let's keep going." And on we went, till we found a hotel in the next town where we could sleep twice for four dollars.

In August of 1950 we were hired to do one TV show for the Dumont Network. We had to go to New York to do the show. I was really excited, because I felt that the show could be a great boost for us.

The show came off very well. There weren't all that many TV sets, or even stations nationwide yet, but we heard that many people had watched us.

Our first dance job after the TV program took us to the Statler Hotel in Washington, D.C. The review in the Washington paper the following morning was very uncomplimentary. The writer called us "a corny band playing stale beer-hall music." I thought that the bad review would upset Lawrence, but he just laughed and said, "As long as they write something, that's the main thing!"

A few years later, when we were much better established in TV and recording, we were called upon to entertain at the inaugural ball for President Eisenhower. At one point in the evening, Ike asked us to play "The Yellow Rose of Texas." Lawrence turned to us and asked anyone who knew it to please lead the band into the number. Well, I played it as I remembered it from my childhood days, but it was apparently the wrong "Yellow Rose"!

The next day, we made every paper in the country, with headlines reading, "Lawrence Welk Plays Wrong Yellow Rose!"

While we were in the plane on our way home, Lawrence came over to me and said, "Well, you can take the rest of the year off! You've earned your money by getting us into every paper in the country for free!"

The Aragon and KTLA

In January, 1951, a few months after our telecast over the Dumont network, Lawrence was telling Lois Lamont and me about an offer he had received from California: "Sam Lutz has us set for four weeks at the Aragon Ballroom in Ocean Park, California, in May of this year. He has arranged for us to telecast over KTLA, Channel 5, right from the ballroom. I talked to Klaus Landsberg, the manager of KTLA, and he wants us to do our regular program, featuring many of the band members, and they'll televise it. I'm not sure about this, but Sam tells me Mr. Landsberg is a genius when it comes to TV."

"Mr. Welk," I said excitedly, "I think our band is a natural for TV. We feature so many soloists like Roberta Linn, Rocky Rockwell, Garth Andrews, Dick Dale, Jerry Burke, and our own Battles on the Accordion. We're perfect for TV. I can't wait!"

With characteristic persistence and dedication, Lawrence started immediately to prepare himself and the band for new roles as popular dance band members *and* television performers. Of all the "big bands" traveling at that time, Lawrence Welk was the most prepared for television. He specialized in spotlighting the various talents of the band members rather than featuring himself—as did

135

most of the other band leaders like Tommy and Jimmy Dorsey, Harry James, Wayne King, and Woody Herman.

We opened at the Aragon Ballroom the first part of May. Our first TV shows were done on Friday nights. We started the dance music at eight forty-five and did the show for KTLA from nine to ten.

The area in front of the stage was roped off to make room for the cameras that were wheeled around to give different angles. The TV director sat in a closed truck outside the back door of the ballroom and winged the show, that is, he did it live on camera, without rehearsal. We always supplied him with a list of songs scheduled, but he had to use his own educated judgment as to which camera shots to use.

There were about three hundred people in the ballroom to watch our first program; by the fourth week, the crowd had grown to over three thousand! People often stopped us on the streets to say how much they were enjoying the shows. I discovered that TV is a tremendous method of communication and became very thankful for it. Little did I realize that this small beginning would lead to a full generation of exposure on the tube!

The appearances on Channel 5 began to bring in requests for personal appearances. Sam Lutz came to me one day and said I had been requested to appear in Pasadena, California, for the Accordion Teachers Guild (ATG). They were putting on a show featuring some accordion bands from local studios and Anthony Galla-Rini. Sam said he could get a hundred and fifty dollars for me for the afternoon. I was ecstatic! I was going to be paid to appear on the same bill with Galla-Rini—one of the all-time great artists of the accordion, and one of my personal heroes!

I arrived at the Pasadena Civic Auditorium to find cars parked everywhere. I figured it must be a Lawrence

136

Welk date and I had misunderstood Sam, or maybe there was also another event taking place at the same time. As I walked in the stage door, a number of the teachers met me. Their excitement showed in their faces.

"This is the first time we've ever had a sold-out house, and they all came to see you!"

I couldn't believe it! With Galla-Rini on the same program, I was getting the credit for the huge sell-out crowd! I resolved then and there that I would somehow stay on TV forever! That resolve was strengthened later that afternoon when I walked onstage to a tremendous ovation.

The teachers I met that day, who became my fast friends, have helped and encouraged me along the way. Many of them have since passed away, but their dedication to our beloved instrument remains an inspiration to me to this day.

The members of the ATG and the American Accordionists' Association are the moving forces behind the growing popularity of the accordion and the establishment of a library of music for the instrument. One reason the orchestra leader at Augustana College frowned on the "squeeze-box" was the fact that symphony writers had never been aware of the accordion. (In fact, its origins go back only a bit over a century.)

While we were appearing at the Aragon in May 1951, Berdyne felt that certain signs called for a visit to a doctor. We learned that she would be giving birth to a "companion" for Randee around the end of November.

With a new baby on the way, we decided that it would be a good idea to find some place other than a motel to live. We settled on a duplex near the Los Angeles International Airport. Rent was a hundred dollars a month with one extra month's rent as security against damage to the apartment. I didn't like that part of the agreement because it seemed to reflect on Berdyne's skill as a homemaker, and that was beyond reproach. In spite of that, we signed a lease and moved in. In a matter of days the little house had become a home in every sense of the word. I decided, rather smugly, "That two dollars I spent for a marriage license was the best investment I ever made!"

A few months earlier the band had appeared at Elitch's Gardens in Denver, Colorado. While there I became acquainted with Jack Ashton, a salesman for New York Life Insurance. He had many friends in Los Angeles and gave me letters introducing me to Dr. L. J. Paben, who became our dentist, and to Drs. Joe and Karl Frudenfeld, both of whom specialized in obstetrics in Inglewood, California. It was a very lucky coincidence that we should find an apartment so near to such fine doctors.

Berdyne paid a visit to Dr. Frudenfeld a few weeks later. "Yes," Dr. Karl confirmed. "You can expect this new baby around November 22."

I asked if he could guarantee arrival on or before the twenty-second. "No one can tell for sure," he answered. "The baby comes when it's ready—not when we're ready! Why do you ask?"

"My birthday is on the fifth of November," I told him, "I'd kind of like to have another Scorpio in the family."

Dr. Frudenfeld just laughed: "We'll just have to wait and see. You know what they say—what will be, will be."

Our engagement at the Aragon Ballroom was beginning to look like a permanent job. The dances Tuesday through Sunday drew more and more people every week. The TV show (so far without a sponsor) was becoming more and more popular. Magazines began calling for interviews. Soon stories on Lawrence, Roberta Linn, and others in the band were appearing in many of the fan magazines. Mary

Lee Schaefer formed a national fan club for Lawrence and the band. Roberta Linn had her own club and four young ladies wanted to start one for me. The future was really taking shape. Dorothy Reams took over my Good Neighbor Fan Club years later and remains the president, vice president, secretary, treasurer, and general jill-of-all-trades today. Her husband Ralph lends moral support. Thank you, Dorothy.

Always anxious to share my good fortune, I invited Clarence Willard, our first trumpet man, and his wife, Lucille, and several other friends, over to the house for Thanksgiving dinner. I knew that Berdyne was about due to go to the hospital, but since she never complained, there were times when I did not use good sense. She prepared a wonderful dinner; and as we all sat down to eat, I offered a prayer of thanksgiving of my own for our good fortune, and asked that Berdyne and the baby would get through the delivery without any problems.

A couple of hours later, after dinner was over and the kitchen clean, Berdyne said, "Myron, you'd better get me to the hospital soon. I've been timing the contractions for quite a while, and they're getting too close for comfort now."

But Lucille, who knew that Clarence and I were due at the Aragon in just a little over an hour, said, "You fellows go to work. I'll take Berdyne to the hospital."

"Are you sure you'll be all right, Honey!" I asked.

"Go ahead," she answered. "I'll be OK, and it'll probably take a while anyway. You can come to the hospital after work."

We had a very big crowd at the ballroom that evening, and everyone was thrilled when I announced that Berdyne had gone to the hospital to deliver our second baby. When Lawrence left around eleven, the ballroom manager came over to me and said, "You'd better get moving! The hospital just called, and your wife is in the delivery room right now!"

I arrived at the hospital just in time to greet little Kristie Ann as Berdyne was wheeled out of the delivery room holding her.

"You have a beautiful, healthy baby daughter, Myron," Dr. Karl Frudenfeld said, beaming.

I sent a little prayer of thanks to heaven, and heard Berdyne whisper, "Don't throw away that list of names, Honey. Better just file it! Maybe next time it will be a boy. But this time it's Kristie Ann."

How fortunate could a man be?

Our little apartment near the airport was becoming very crowded, so Berdyne and I decided that it was time to buy a home of our own. I had never liked paying rent—it seemed that all I had to show for the rental money was a pile of receipts and a lot of aggravation whenever the landlady made her little "surprise" visits to check the condition of her building.

We found a nice three-bedroom house in Westchester, just a few blocks from the airport. The price was right: about $18,500 with the promise of a $17,000 loan. This would give us plenty of living room, a garage, and a backyard with an avocado tree. Lots of room in the backyard for a playhouse for the girls, too. I could feel my old carpentering urges growing!

The payments on the loan would be only about a hundred and sixty dollars a month with the interest at six percent! We were just getting ready to move in when the real estate agent called to inform us that we didn't qualify for the loan of $17,000 because I was a musician! It seemed that they had a list of forty-three "credit risks"; musicians were number forty-two on that list. The bank was willing

140

to loan me $15,000, but for twenty years—not twenty-five—and that would mean bigger payments. I took a deep breath and allowed as how that would be no problem. We really needed that house! "Who's at the bottom of that list?" I asked, just out of curiosity.

"Traveling salesmen," they answered. Well!!!

We had also applied for mortgage insurance, but once again could not qualify because of my profession and health problems.

"Don't worry about that," Berdyne said when I told her about the insurance. "They don't know you like I do!"

Although I was a "TV star" we were still not rolling in money so we decided to paint the house ourselves.

At the Aragon I had met Mark and Ann Humes, who owned a paint and wallpaper store in Bellflower, about twenty-five miles from our new home. Their daughter, Helen Carol, was very interested in the accordion, so we all quickly became good friends. Mark and Ann were at the ballroom the night Berdyne and I decided on the house, and they suggested that we come to their store for a good price on all the supplies we would need. My first reaction was that twenty-five miles was an awful long way to drive for paint! But then, I thought, the paint store owners in our area might not be accordion lovers either! So a few days later, we drove to their store and spent the morning picking out paints, brushes, rollers, thinners, and wallpaper.

"Who's going to do the painting for you?" Mark asked as he wrote out our order.

"Thought I would do it myself," I answered. "I've done a little painting in my time, and I think it might be fun."

"Well, that sounds OK," Mark said. "We'll bring everything over to you on Sunday, if that's all right."

We agreed that Sunday would be fine and then started

on the long drive home.

"Wonder why they want to bring it over on Sunday?" Berdyne mused.

"Well, I suppose the store is closed and they saw our car was too small to hold all that paint."

The following Saturday night was especially busy at the Aragon, and by the time I got home—well after 2 A.M.— I was more than ready for a good, long sleep. Early the next morning, though, I was awakened from a wonderful dream of encore after encore by Berdyne, who had already fed Randee and Kristie. She shook me awake, saying, "The people from the paint store are here, and they've brought all the supplies plus some of their friends! You'd better get up right away!"

Sure enough, it was Mark and Ann Humes along with their business partners Mike and Helen Seiler and Dorothy and Gene Nichols.

"We didn't have anything to do today," Mark said as I stood rubbing the sleep out of my eyes. "So we decided to come over here and do a little painting."

And I thought those things only happened in storybooks!

Soon, with Randee giving her expert three-year-old help, and Kristie just looking on in wonder, the paint began to fly. Our new neighbors, the Condors and the Hodges, brought coffee, lemonade, and sweet rolls. By suppertime the whole house had been painted—inside and out! Berdyne and I hugged everyone tightly. From then on we were sure California would be our home forever! Mark and Ann did many wonderful things for us over the years. One of the most memorable and certainly the luckiest was introducing us to Dr. Edward Hackie and his wife Joan. Without Dr. Hackie's common sense approach to illness this particular story might have had a much different ending.

Our TV shows on KTLA were becoming more and more popular. Sponsors, the lifeblood of television, were beginning to notice us. Laura Scudder Potato Chips was the first to approach Lawrence about sponsoring his shows.

"I don't see why we should pay so much for your show," the Laura Scudder agent said to Lawrence. "We never heard of you until the past few weeks—even though the ratings are good!"

And Lawrence (God bless him!) answered, "Well, we'll start out even then, because I've never heard of you either!"

Roberta Linn was becoming a star in her own right, and when Mr. Landsberg offered her a show of her own, she was ecstatic. He also wanted me on the show, but I felt that my loyalties were with Lawrence. And besides, I was satisfied where I was.

Many local columnists predicted the end of Lawrence Welk when Roberta left us. One in particular delighted in taking potshots at me, saying he couldn't stand all the smiling. "No one could be that happy!" was his claim. I never did let him in on the secret; I decided to just let him find out for himself. I was (and *am!*) so happy doing what I'm doing that I can't help smiling. It sure beats working for a living!

It was time to find a new Champagne Lady. The publicity and the search really helped our ratings, and as Lawrence had said in Washington, D.C., "Let them write whatever they want as long as they spell your name right."

Now *that's* a problem I've had all along. My name has been spelled Florin, Florian, Florien, and Florence...

143

even Florenzo once, by a journalist who thought that an accordionist just had to have an Italian background. Guess I'll just have to keep on working till they all get it right!

Our long search finally turned up Alice Lon of Dallas, Texas—and a prettier, more vivacious Champagne Lady would have been very hard to find!

Alice and I shared many personal appearances as part of the publicity campaign heralding her first performances with the band. Once, after appearing at a department store Christmas party in San Diego, our return flight to L.A. was badly delayed by a heavy fog. When we finally landed in Burbank, thirty miles out of the way, it was already five-thirty in the afternoon. We had to be at the Aragon Ballroom by eight for that evening's TV show! My car was at Los Angeles International Airport, so we took a taxi there, grabbed my car, and hurried to my house in Westchester to clean up. At seven o'clock we ran from the house and jumped back into my car for the twenty-minute drive to the ballroom. About fifteen minutes later I realized we were lost in a heavy fog that reminded me very much of the pea-soup fogs I had seen in London.

At last I got my bearings—after many minutes of aimless wandering—and got us to the ballroom with just minutes to spare. I quickly removed the accordion from its case and ran on stage just as the stage manager shouted, "Ten seconds!" My solo, the second number on the program, was "Get Me to the Church on Time"!

The show, of course, went off without a hitch, and afterward I approached Lawrence to apologize for any worry that I may have caused him. To my surprise, he just said, "I wasn't worried. I knew that you would make it on time."

Love that man!!

32. Our surprise 10th Wedding Anniversary party at the Buggy Whip Restaurant in Westchester, California.

33. (*Above*) The Buckeye Four (St. Louis 1946–50). L–R: Si Wilkins, "Horseshoe" Mike Riaff, "Cowboy" Joe Randall, and Yours Truly.
34. (*Below*) The Buckeye Four (back row) with Tommy Sutton, Mary Lou Sutton, and Charlie Ackerson.

35. Daddy with Randee.

36. (*Above*) Lawrence Welk with his Champagne Music Makers (1950). L–R. Back row: Lawrence Welk, Champagne Lady Roberta Linn, Whistler Roy Woldum, Barney Liddell, Curt Ramsey, Clarence Willard, "Gus" George Thow, Nicky Aden, Bob Pilot, Jerry Burke. Front row: Garth Andrews, George Willard, George Aubry, Orie Amadeo, Clark Gandy, "Guess Who?" with the accordion, and Larry Hooper.

37. (*Below*) Roberta Linn and me entertaining Army patients at Fitzsimmons General Hospital in Denver.

38. (*Left*) Randee and Kristie with their proud parents, 1952.

39. (*Below*) This is the first publicity picture of Lawrence Welk and me. 1950. *Photo by James J. Kriegsmann, N.Y.*

41. Hamming it up at the Aragon while Lawrence Welk and Jerry Burke grin in the background.

40. (*Left*) The Champagne Music Makers celebrating their second anniversary at the Aragon Ballroom, 1953. L–R. Back row: George Aubry, Jerry Burke, Barney Liddell, Harry Lewis (our arranger), Curt Ramsey, Bob Pilot, Dick Kesner, Dick Dale, Garth Andrews, Larry Hooper. 2nd row: Alice Lon (Champagne Lady), Lawrence Welk, Rocky Rockwell, Bill Page, Clarence Willard, Yours Truly, Johnny Klein, Lois Lamont (secretary), Orie Amadeo. Kneeling left: Bob Lido and Norman Bailey. Kneeling right: Gene Purcell and Aladdin.

42. (*Below*) With my five beautiful girls and their mother. L–R: Holly, Heidi, Randee (standing), Berdyne, Kristie, and Robin. 1965. *Photo by Bob Plunkett.*

43. (*Above*) Berdyne and I were so happy when Kristie and Bobby Burgess were married in February 1971. *Photo by Bob Plunkett.*

44. (*Below*) The program when I played the wrong "Yellow Rose of Texas."

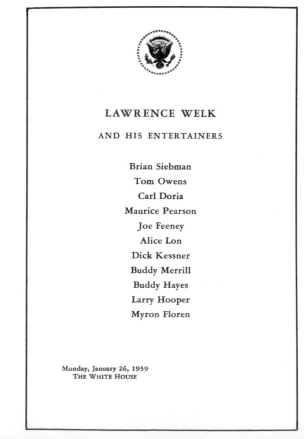

LAWRENCE WELK

AND HIS ENTERTAINERS

Brian Siebman

Tom Owens

Carl Doria

Maurice Pearson

Joe Feeney

Alice Lon

Dick Kessner

Buddy Merrill

Buddy Hayes

Larry Hooper

Myron Floren

Monday, January 26, 1959
THE WHITE HOUSE

45. (*Above*) It's not work when you have five lovely daughters helping you. Planting a tree Arbor Day, 1966, at the Rolling Hills Arboretum. Supervisor Kenneth Hahn of Los Angeles is directing the planting. *Photo by L.A. Chamber of Commerce.*

46. (*Below left*) A very gracious lady. Doris Tirrell with Walter Lendh and me. *Photo by Bauman Photography, Inc., Brockton, Massachusetts.*

47. (*Below right*) In April 1977 the town of Roslyn honored me with this sign and special events.

48. (*Above left*) With my best girl. *Photo by Paul Walker, Coeur d'Alene, Idaho.*
49. (*Above right*) June 22, 1980, the wedding day of Heidi to Sam Gennowey. *Photo by Paul Walker, Coeur d'Alene, Idaho.*
50. (*Below left*) Grandson Robert Floren Burgess at 20 months.
51. (*Below right*) Granddaughter Becki Jane Burgess at 4 years.

52. (*Left*) Grandchildren are such fun. Here's Robert Burgess looking over the shoulder of a friend. *Photo by Niki Mareschal.*

53. (*Below*) And Becki Jane with her daddy, Christmas 1980 on the Lawrence Welk Show. *Photo by Niki Mareschal.*

54. (*Left*) Practicing for the annual Wurstfest in New Braunfels, Texas. *Photo by Paul Walker, Coeur d'Alene, Idaho.*

55. (*Below*) Heidi (Miss "Loverwurst") with me in 1980 for my 13th consecutive year entertaining at the Wurstfest in New Braunfels, Texas. *Photo by Wurstfest Association.*

56. Son-in-law Bobby Burgess with Elaine Niverson, his dancing partner. *Photo by Eric Skipsey*

57. It's always a pleasure to accompany the beautiful voice of lovely Norma Zimmer. *Photo by Niki Mareschal.*

58. (*Above*) Bobby and Elaine accompanied by an accordion player on the Welk show. *Photo by Niki Mareschal.*
59. (*Below*) Lawrence Welk conducts the Champagne Music Makers, 1981. *Photo by Niki Mareschal.*

60. (*Above left*) Daughter Holly and I enjoy a daily jog. *Photo by Paul Walker, Coeur d'Alene, Idaho.*

61. (*Above right*) Randee Floren (now Mrs. McGooey) with her husband, Jack.

62. (*Below*) Sister Cabrini and Sister Canice at Our Lady of Assumption Convent keep close guard over my accordion after it was stolen in Wisconsin.

Lawrence was becoming very busy with the business aspects of a successful TV band and soon hired George Cates to help with rehearsals. George's background with Decca Records and the Russ Morgan Band were very impressive, and even though he sometimes grated on the nerves of the musicians, he always managed to get just the sound Lawrence wanted out of the band. I've always been grateful to George, not just musically, but also for the kindness he showed to my friend GI Joe a few years later.

Thanks to our growing popularity, Lawrence decided that it was time to expand the band by adding strings. One of the first new members was Bob Lido, who is still with us today. Bob is a tremendous musician and at that time had been with the Carmen Cavallero Band. He is a very quiet man, but onstage he is a dynamic performer. Aladdin Pallante joined us at the same time, and the two of them made a wonderful pair for TV. Their Italian version of "Darktown Strutters' Ball" still brings me a happy feeling.

Aladdin, a devout Catholic, passed away a few years ago. We all still miss him and his effervescent sense of humor. A joke he told me one day was typical of his humor:

The Catholic Church was having difficulty selecting a new pope. Finally they narrowed the choice down to one Monsignor Secola. The vote was almost unanimous... except for one lone voice from the back of the room: "Wait! How would it sound? Pope Secola??"

Aladdin had previously been a member of Xavier Cugat's band, and was really pleased at the chance to do TV. TV, though, had some dangerous moments for Aladdin. He and Bob Lido were playing bricklayers one evening. On cue, Aladdin was to walk through the newly finished wall of bricks and knock it down. Everything

145

worked fine during rehearsal, but when the time came for the live performance, Aladdin walked through the wall, slipped in a puddle of water, and fell flat on his back... knocking himself out cold! He just lay there. When we broke for a commercial, we revived him with smelling salts. But he refused to go to a hospital to be checked over till after the show was over!

Larry Hooper, our bass singer and pianist, was becoming so popular that Lawrence decided to feature him on nearly every show. One day our recording director brought in a new song, "O Happy Day," that seemed to be tailor-made for "Hoopy."

He sang it on one show and it became an instant hit—and added to the feeling that Lawrence Welk and his Champagne Music Makers were becoming a force in TV. George Cates had a hit record at this time, too. It was a combination of the theme from *Picnic* and a song called "Moonglow." It was so good, we still use it today.

Dick Kesner became the third member of our string section, and as usual with the people that Lawrence chose, he became a special favorite of our viewers. Dick had a kind of Fritz Kreisler look, and he played lovely, simple, melodic songs that the audience loved. I had acquired the title of The Happy Norwegian, so Dick decided to refer to himself as The Sour Kraut.

Singer-saxophone player Dick Dale and his wife, Marguerite, came from Algona, Iowa, to join the band in early 1951. They quickly became Berdyne's and my good friends, and in the early years we got together socially quite a bit.

That same year we heard that we might be chosen as a summer replacement show for Dodge. Ina Ray Hutton and her all-girl band were also being considered. I remember some of those first meetings with Bert Carter and Jack

146

Minor of the Chrysler Corporation. Bert was a veteran of the company and Jack, a brash young executive with a million ideas for selling cars. The advertising agency sent over a man by the name of John Gaunt to attend these meetings. One day, during a break in the meeting, I asked John how they planned to do the show.

"Well," he answered, "besides the band, we'll have a comedian and a line of dancing girls."

Lawrence overheard this and broke in: "Not with my band. If you insist on a comedian and dancing girls, count me out. My fans would never accept me that way."

Lawrence sure knew (and still knows) his audience!

The ABC Network

Our first network show sponsored by Dodge on ABC was scheduled for July 2, 1955. We were considered something of a curiosity by the other people at the studio, but I felt that we were destined to be an even bigger hit on the network than we were on local television in Los Angeles. Jack Minor of the Chrysler Corporation came to see the final rehearsal and OK'd all the numbers. The only one I remember today was my solo, "Tico Tico," still one of my favorites. The show was panned pretty badly by the critics, but the public response was very encouraging. Once again, we all heard Lawrence say, "Let them print what they want as long as they spell your names correctly."

Jack Minor felt that we could use a boost in the ratings, so he arranged a musical tour of the country to promote the show. We would appear in conjunction with the local Dodge dealers in Houston, Dallas, San Antonio, and Philadelphia on this first tour. Everywhere we went, the crowds were tremendous, and the dealers were wild with enthusiasm. They met us at the airport in each city and drove us to our show location in a police-escorted motorcade of Dodge cars with our names printed on the sides. Our ratings improved steadily after each tour. At the end of the summer, Dodge decided that they would continue to sponsor us through the winter and then would decide if the arrangement would become permanent.

Most of the critics picked on Lawrence's accented English and his mispronunciation of words like *wonderful,* which came out "wunnerful." One of his favorite expressions after a good performance was "Wunnerful...ah... wunnerful!" Soon it seemed as if everyone in the country was using that same expression. Lawrence thought maybe he should work on improving his English, but Don Fedderson (or "Featherson" as Lawrence would say) and Sam Lutz suggested that he forget that idea: "If you lose your accent we could lose the show!"

Stan Freberg made a record kidding Lawrence and our show. It featured Stony Stonewall (Rocky Rockwell), Larry Looper (Larry Hooper), the Lemon Sisters (The Lennon Sisters), and all the other "Bubbles." Lawrence got a big kick out of it—especially since he knew that the good-natured kidding could only increase our ratings. The record was a big hit for Stan, and it became another step on Lawrence's climb to the top.

When Sid Caeser did a take-off on the "Lawrence Welk Show" on his own "Show of Shows," and then Lawrence was asked to make an appearance on the "Jack Benny Show," we felt we had at last really arrived at the top. Guest shots with Lucille Ball and "This is Your Life" were icing on the cake!

In 1953 we enrolled Randee in kindergarten at Chapel of Peace Lutheran Elementary School in Inglewood, California. We had chosen that church a couple of years earlier when Sandy and Eunice Sandahl, old friends from South Dakota, invited us to join. We felt very much at home with the membership of the church since it was made up mostly of midwestern "transplants" like ourselves.

150

Three-year-old Kristie was finally beginning to talk...constantly. We had worried a little when she had been approaching two before she had started to talk—after all, Randee started before she was ten months! I reminded Kristie of that a few months ago, and she answered, "Oh, I could talk all right. But I never had anything to say, so I kept quiet."

I think there may be a lesson there for a lot of us!

Berdyne was feeling "that way" again, and on July 1, 1954, Robin Gay was born. Now we had three daughters—I felt that my cup was indeed running over! Berdyne's father had passed away a few years earlier, and her mother, Albena Koerner, had come out from South Dakota to live with us. (Incidentally, no one will ever hear mother-in-law jokes from me! Albena is the greatest!) With six members of our family now in residence in our little Westchester house, things were becoming a little crowded. I decided that since our future on TV was looking very good, this would be a good time to look for a larger home. After a couple of months of searching, we found a big, roomy house in Windsor Hills, not far from the ABC studios. We moved there in September of 1954. This time we had no problem with financing!

My folks arrived for a visit a few weeks later, and they loved our new home. We were just beginning to really enjoy their company when I noticed that Pa was having trouble with a sore on his neck. When I asked him about it, he answered that it was nothing much, but it just didn't seem to want to heal. He had not seen a doctor, so I asked him to come along with me when I visited Dr. Hackie for a checkup.

When my examination was finished, I asked Dr. Hackie to take a look at Pa's neck. He did—for quite a

151

while—and then became very quiet. He walked to the window and looked out for a long time before facing us. (Dr. Hackie puts on a gruff appearance, and he doesn't pull punches when it comes to hard facts, but it seems to hurt him more than the patient when he has to give bad news.)

"Mr. Floren, you have cancer. It's a good thing we've discovered it now. Radium treatments should take care of it. Go to the hospital in Long Beach and see the cancer specialists."

Pa was very upset, of course. "What if I don't go?" he asked.

"Then you have at most a year to live."

"And if I *do* go for treatment?"

"Ten to fifteen years maybe."

Pa turned to me then and said, "As long as we're halfway there, let's get going right now!"

Cancer. The word alone sent cold chills through me. Our family had always been blessed with good health, and the idea that the "Big C" was present was repugnant to me. I thanked God that the folks had come for a visit at this particular time, and that we had had the good fortune to meet Dr. Hackie. The cancerous sore was treated and healed. Ten years would pass before we would hear that horrible word again, and then with terrifying results.

We were still making tours all over the country to promote our show. Frequently I would be away from home for weeks on end and come back to find that the girls had grown *inches* while I was gone. I've always been glad that Albena was home with Berdyne and the kids, and that we had so many wonderful, close friends. Those years would have been much lonelier for me on the road—and especially for Berdyne at home—without all of them.

Additions to the band seemed at times to be almost foreordained. Jim Roberts, who joined us shortly before we went network, became the ladies' favorite. From Madison-ville, Kentucky, he was—and is—a great gentleman. I'm sometimes mistaken for Jimmy by weaker-eyed fans, and I'm happy to accept the extra attention.

Lawrence's timing is uncanny; he even knows when to be sick! He was in bed with a cold one day when his son, Larry, Jr., brought a quartet of young ladies home from school to entertain him. Janet, nine; Kathy, eleven; Peggy, thirteen; and Diane, sixteen—The Lennon Sisters—imme-diately thrilled Lawrence and, on their first show with us, captured the fancy of the audience. They became one of the mainstays of the show, and it was such a pleasure to watch the girls grow up into beautiful, accomplished young women. Their simple, barbershop harmonies were just the thing to complement the champagne music and polkas on our show.

Alice Lon was becoming very popular—and famous for her many-skirted petticoats that would flare out when she danced the polka with Lawrence.

In 1957 Joe Feeney made his first appearance with the band. Joe, who is from Grand Island, Nebraska, never fails to please the fans with his beautiful—and very powerful—Irish tenor voice. Once, when Joe and I did a show together at a theater in the Midwest, Joe was in especially good voice that evening as we strolled through the audience. The whole audience was entranced with his singing and, except for our music, the theater was silent. Then Joe reached the phrase "a little bit of heaven fell," and as he lingered on *fell*, about a hundred steel folding chairs that had been perched precariously in the orchestra pit crashed to the floor. Now, how could I follow that?!

In 1959 Champagne Music was rolling along. Our ratings were improving every week. What could possibly add to our happiness? Berdyne supplied the answer. A

Fourth-of-July baby. Holly Jean was born the evening of July fourth just as the usual display of fireworks burst above the coliseum. The happy sound of the exploding pyrotechnics matched my own feelings.

From 1958 to 1960 we added several more artists to our group. Buddy Merrill with his boyish smile and excellent guitar work was very popular. Russ Klein in the saxophone section and Kenny Trimble in the trombone section were also great assets. Jack Imel joined us in 1959. He started as a marimba player and tap dancer and later became a valuable member of our production staff. Today, Jack's dance specialty numbers with Mary Lou Metzger are a very popular part of our weekly shows.

Jack occasionally got into little problem situations in his early days—problems that can cause listeners to literally fall on the floor laughing. He has a habit of venting his feelings in a wild, apelike roar...often with little or no warning anything was about to happen. A few years ago we were booked into the Rose Festival in Portland, Oregon. We arrived at our hotel about eleven o'clock on a beautiful, clear morning. Jack was so tickled to be in the fresh, clean air of Portland that he opened the window of his tenth-floor room and let go with one of his better bellows. Feeling exhilarated and just about to throw out another yell, he looked down to see a painter on a scaffold directly below his window. The painter was frozen in position, the paintbrush dripping paint down his outstretched arm and into his shocked face. Stunned, Jack drew back from his window to collect his thoughts.

"What have I done?" he thought. "That guy could fall and kill himself after a scare like that!"

Jack rushed back to the window to apologize, only to find an empty scaffold—the man was nowhere to be seen.

Later that day, as we were leaving for the show, we

heard from behind closed doors in the hotel office downstairs, "Get somebody else to do your painting. You have lunatics staying here!"

Jim Hobson and Ed Sobol were our director and producer on the early shows. Jim had worked with Don Fedderson on the "Liberace Show," and Ed was an old-time producer. Ed passed away in the early sixties, but Jim is still with us today.

In 1959 we signed with Dot Records, owned by Randy Wood. Other labels, including Victor, Columbia, and Decca were also bidding for our recording contracts, but Lawrence finally decided on Randy Wood—mostly because of his promise to get us a hit record by the end of a year.

That's when "Calcutta" (no relation to *Oh Calcutta!*) appeared on the scene. Randy wanted us to use JoAnn Castle, our honkey-tonk-piano gal, on the record, but Lawrence and George Cates had just "discovered" the harpsichord and decided it would be best to go with a "new" sound. With Frank Scott playing the "harpsi" and myself on the accordion, a vocal octet and rhythm section, we made the record. Record sales picked right up after we played the number on the show. Randy Wood worked night and day to get air time for the song on the radio; but he kept stressing that TV exposure was much more important.

Now we had to figure out ways to use that song almost every week without making it seem like just another commercial. Remember what I said about timing? Lawrence had been thinking of adding a dance couple to the show. One of the first couples to try out was nineteen-year-old Bobby Burgess and his partner, Barbara Boylan. Bobby had spent several years working for Lawrence's old friend Walt Disney on the "Mickey Mouse Club," and now

155

he had worked out a dance number for "Calcutta." Bobby and Barbara were added to our list of entertainers, and each and every week they came up with a new dance to the same music.

Eventually, "Calcutta" earned a place among the million sellers with sales in excess of 1,600,000 singles and 600,000 albums. I can still thank that recording for introducing me to the first of my four sons-in-law!

Lawrence has always loved dixieland music, and he was really pleased when Pete Fountain from New Orleans agreed to join us. As with the Lennon Sisters, it was Larry, Jr., who first brought Pete to Lawrence's attention. Pete's outgoing personality brought many happy times to the band. He was too much of a soloist to really master the techniques of playing with the saxophone section. As he said, "I never let the notes interfere with my playing!" Lawrence quickly decided to capitalize on Pete's individuality by featuring him in as many solo spots as possible.

When Pete first appeared on the show, he was bald. And for some reason, we received a lot of unfavorable letters about that, so, after a couple weeks in Hollywood, he suddenly appeared with a full head of hair.

Not long after Pete started "wearing hair" we played an outdoor concert in Red Rock, near Denver, Colorado. I was conducting the orchestra in "My Fair Lady" when the wind suddenly came up and blew all our music off the stands and scattered it all over the amphitheater. I was more than a little worried about Pete's new hair—he was due to perform next, and the wind was getting stronger. But as soon as he appeared, I knew that I would never again underestimate the ingenuity of a Louisiana boy! He had borrowed a pretty red ribbon from one of the girls and had tied it over his head and under his chin! As he

156

played, his hair flapped up and down in the wind, but it never did leave his head!

Pete left us to return to his home in New Orleans after just a couple of years. But his recordings and the funny memories he left behind are as fresh today as ever. Along with Mardi Gras, Pete Fountain typifies the great Dixie heritage of New Orleans.

Reprise—GI Joe

Nineteen fifty-five. Life had been kind to Berdyne and me. We were living in our second home in Los Angeles, and our girls were growing up fast. Randee was six, Kristie, three, and Robin was just one year old.

We had finished our live show at ABC at seven o'clock, and I was rushing on my way to the Aragon for the Saturday evening dance program.

As always, I gulped down the supper Berdyne had ready for me when I stopped at home between shows. I noticed Randee and Kristie watching me from the kitchen doorway. They seemed amazed at how fast food would disappear whenever Daddy was around!

"What kind of pie was that?" Berdyne asked as I finished the last bite.

I thought fast. It was so good—I knew I'd had that kind before. But what was it? I thought, "Mind! Don't fail me now!"

I took a wild guess. "Peach?" As soon as the word was out, I knew I'd goofed.

"Guess again, Daddy," Randee and Kristie giggled.

"He'll never guess. It's his favorite: rhubarb," Berdyne said smiling at the girls. "At least he said it was his favorite when he used to have it back home on the farm."

"Well, whatever it was, I loved it. It was the best peach-rhubarb pie you ever made!" I said to her.

"Too late for flattery," Berdyne laughed. "By the way, do you know a Joe H——?"

"No, I don't think so," I answered. "Why?"

"Well, he called here this afternoon and said he knew you when you were in Europe during the war. He wants you to call him at the Roosevelt Hotel. He spoke with an English accent."

My mind raced. It couldn't be! Or could it?

I dialed the number Berdyne had written down, and asked for the room number noted on the pad.

"Hello. Joe H—— speaking." I was stunned! It was the same voice, but deeper and touched by a beautiful Australian-English accent.

"Joe," I said, "this is Myron Floren."

"Myron! This is your old friend GI Joe from Germany!" I heard his voice through the memories that were flooding over me. "I came to America to see you. I talked to your wife this afternoon; she sounds like a wonderful lady! You are a lucky man."

"Joe, you don't know how lucky I am! And now that I've heard from you, my prayers have been answered again." Then I added, "How did you find me?"

"It's a long story, and one with a happy ending. When can I see you and your family?"

"I'm heading for the Aragon right now, but tomorrow we're doing a telethon at KTLA for the Arthritis Foundation. The studio is right near your hotel in Hollywood. Why don't you come and meet me there?"

As I drove to the ballroom that evening, a flood of memories washed over me. GI Joe, alive! And here he was in California to see me! Life has a way of coming up with surprises at the strangest times!

160

I left early for KTLA the next afternoon. When I arrived a guard met me, saying, "There's a fellow waiting for you in the office. He says he knew you in Europe."

Joe saw me talking with the guard and hurried toward me. I stared at him. Bigger and heavier, about twenty-six or twenty-seven now, but unmistakeably GI Joe. He still had that same wide grin and unruly mop of black hair. We embraced strongly. For a minute I couldn't speak. I could feel my eyes smart with tears—not of sadness, but of happiness. I introduced Joe to the band members as they arrived, and also to George Cates and Sam Lutz. George and Sam took an immediate liking to Joe—especially when they discovered their common Jewish heritage and Joe's experiences in Germany. On our way back to Windsor Hills after the telethon, Joe filled me in on the years since 1945.

"About three months after you left, I was allowed to go to Israel and enter school. I was a little old for school, but I needed to learn a trade, so I decided to go anyway. When I graduated from high school, I spent a few years as a dental technician. The government of Australia was advertising for adventurous people to settle in their great nation. It was like the last frontier. It sounded like a chance to make my fortune so I moved to Melbourne and opened a factory. I worked hard, made a lot of money and finally had many factories. Now I've decided to go to Israel for a while. But first I wanted to find my old friend, Myron Floren!"

"But," I broke in, "how did you ever find me? This is a big country!"

And then he told me about a piece of detective work that would have made Sherlock Holmes proud!

"Well, I know my friend, Myron Floren, is an entertainer; so naturally I must come to Hollywood, where all

161

entertainers in America are sure to live. I have this picture of us in Europe, and I start showing it to everyone I meet. Finally after about three days, I meet an accordion player who knows you and he gives me your telephone number!"

Talk about Divine Providence! Imagine going into a strange country aided only by a twelve-year-old picture ... and then finding the person you want to see within days!

I recognized that drive in Joe when I first met him at the hotel in Schwerin. I sense the same ambition in Lawrence Welk. When they set out to do something, nothing can stop them. Hearing the words "it can't be done" only intensifies their determination.

Proudly I introduced Joe to my family. I had never told Berdyne about Joe, and as he told his story, she and the girls were fascinated. They all hit it off like old friends, and Joe got a piece of the "peach" pie.

Joe left for New York the next day with a letter to George Cates's family so he'd have friends when he got there. "Goodbye, Myron," he said. "I hope we'll meet again. *Shalom*."

"*Shalom*, Joe," I echoed. "Be careful. I know we will meet again somewhere."

And he was gone again.

Nineteen sixty. The decade of the fifties had been a most happy one for Berdyne and me. My job with Lawrence Welk had proved to be happy beyond my expectations. We had added three more daughters. My health seemed to be improving year by year and the future had never looked better. We wondered what the sixties would hold.

I didn't have long to wait. On Valentine's Day Berdyne mentioned that I had better think about getting the crib out again. "You'll have time to get it ready because about the end of October we're going to have another deduction."

Heidi Lynne made her debut on October 29.

Five daughters, I thought happily. What could be more perfect? It would have been nice to have a few sons but this way my daughters would bring me sons-in-law that would grace our family and bring us happiness. Thank you, Lord.

Nineteen sixty-five. Eight years have passed, and I find myself standing in the backyard of our new house in Rolling Hills, a suburb about twenty-five miles outside of L.A. Berdyne and I have five daughters now; Holly, who is eight years old, and Heidi, five, are the latest additions to our family. The "Lawrence Welk Show" is doing better than ever; our weekly Saturday night dances are at the Hollywood Palladium now. I figure I must be the luckiest accordion player in the world ... and with that thought, I suddenly find myself thinking of my old friend GI Joe.

Just then the phone rings. I answer and hear, "Hello! This is GI Joe again. I want you to meet my wife. We are on our way to Sweden."

Amazed, I say, "Come right on over! I have a few additions for you to meet, too!"

We have another wonderful visit. Joe has been very lucky in business. He and his wife are already living off his factories and seeing the world.

"Myron, can I do anything for you?" he asks.

"Joe, you have already done more for me than you could ever know! God bless you and your lovely wife!"

It's been fifteen years since we last heard from Joe, but one of these days the phone will ring and that same happy voice will say, as if only a couple of days have passed, "Hello, Myron. This is your old friend GI Joe again!"

Shalom, Joe. Wherever you may be.

The Accordion Man

I'm late for a dance job with Lawrence Welk! Everything is going wrong. I can't find my trousers; there are buttons missing from my shirt; my trousers haven't come back from the cleaners; and the car won't start! Worst of all... *where* is my accordion?!

After many frustrating delays, I finally get to the ballroom—only to find that the job is almost over and people are leaving. Someone asks, "Where was the accordion man tonight?" The answer is so vague, I can't make it out. The band is playing the last song of the evening, "Far Away Places." I can feel my whole world collapsing around me!

Suddenly I realize that the music is coming from my clock radio. Thank God—it was only a dream. It's February 25, 1981, six-thirty in the morning, according to the disc jockey. A few minutes pass before I'm sure that I'm home in my own bed.

Still only half awake, I slip out of bed and walk to the bathroom, where I pull on an old pair of blue jeans, old shoes, and my FFA* jacket. Then I open the back door

*Future Farmers of America

quietly, so as not to disturb Berdyne, who is still sound asleep on her side of the bed.

On my way past the swimming pool, I notice I have company this morning; our little dog, Honey, the product of many years of canine intermarriage, has decided to join me on my walk down to the barn.

"Let's go feed Charro, Honey," I say as she yelps and jumps up and down by the patio door. When I open the gate, she's off like a shot down the driveway to the corral.

Charro, our aging quarter horse, is waiting for me at the door of the barn. Can't fool him! He knows just where those oats are kept—sometimes I'd swear he knows the combination to the lock, too!

After a little clean-up work around the barn, I jog back up the driveway past the house to the mailbox— about two hundred yards—to pick up the *Los Angeles Times* and the *Wall Street Journal*. On the way back to the kitchen door, I pass our twenty-three-year-old daughter Holly. She's on her way to her first class of the day at Redlands University, about seventy miles away. She's a senior, and when she graduates in June, she'll have earned her bachelor's degree in psychology. I wonder if she knows how proud we all are of her? As she climbs into her Jeep, I wish her a good morning and then add, "Take it easy today. Don't do anything I wouldn't do!"

"Don't worry, Dad," she laughs. "I'm so busy with school, that even if my 'Calvins' could talk, they'd have nothing to say!"

Berdyne and I are proud of all our daughters. Typical parents. I had hoped at one time that our family might be evenly divided with maybe three sons and three daughters but fate decreed five daughters. I couldn't be happier. Randee, with a responsible position with the phone company and writing in her spare time; Kristie, a happy house-

166

wife with two children; Robin, also with the phone company and holding a degree in psychology from the University of California; and Heidi, becoming used to being a housewife and doing a little selling in her spare time. Each with her own distinct personality—happy, healthy young women.

Back in the kitchen, I measure out coffee for ten cups in our Mr. Coffee maker—a present eighteen months ago from Randee and Jack.

As the coffee begins to perk, I check the *Wall Street Journal* and find that the market is up again in heavy trading. I glance at some of the stocks I have invested in: American Airlines is up 1¼ to 11¼...well, at least I'm holding my own there; I bought it for 11 in 1965. National Growth Stocks are up four cents at $8.68—if I sold that today, I could declare a long-term capital loss of over $10,000. Why didn't I sell it in 1973 when it rose to over $13? I think sadly of Summers Gyroscope, which became Electronics Capital, which became Shelter Resources. I bought in at 10, watched it go up to 70, and then rode it back down to 3. Today's quote is 2½—I could sell it all and make almost enough money to buy a three-pound can of coffee! Well, you can't win them all!

Speaking of coffee...it's through perking. I pour two cups: one black for Berdyne, and one with a little low-fat milk (for character) for me. As I carry the coffee back into the bedroom, I meet Albena (Berdyne's mother) and Art (her stepfather) coming out of their room. They spend every winter with us to avoid the snow in South Dakota.

"Coffee's ready," I tell them.

"Good," they both answer at once.

"That's the best thing I've heard all day," Albena says. Then she adds, "You're home today? Thought you were supposed to be in Florida!"

"Nope, Florida's tomorrow," I answer. "I'll be catching a plane out of town tonight after taping."

Berdyne is sitting up in bed, watching the news on TV. Reagan is taking confident hold in Washington. He seems to be getting a good start, and I hope that we are indeed embarking on a new era of growth and optimism in our great country. Today the news is full of muggings, robberies, murders—I wonder if we are going to become a nation full of paranoid, frightened people? Do we have to arm ourselves with protective weapons to safeguard our homes? I tell Berdyne again of the many cities where we are warned never to go outside alone in the daytime... and not to go out *at all* at night. I hope the new administration in Washington will help us gain a greater sense of pride in ourselves. I still feel that America is on the threshold of exciting new times.

"What's your schedule today?" I ask. "Are you going to your art class?" Berdyne has been taking classes in oil painting and doing a wonderful job. She has great talent for painting, and a good eye for form and color. Sometimes I kid her, saying that, when her paintings start really selling, I will be able to retire.

"You? Retire?" she answers. "I can't imagine you ever retiring, but I do wish that you would slow down a little. You're not getting any younger, you know. You ought to start taking things a little easier!"

"Well, Honey," I say, "I know I'm not fifty anymore, but I feel better than ever. Besides, music is one profession you can stay in till you die. I'd like to keep going another hundred years!"

"Yes, I suppose you would. But I'm not getting any younger either. It would be nice if we could be together a little more. After all, people are always telling me to make

168

you slow down. I get tired of hearing that—there's nothing I can do about it!"

"Honey, to me you'll never be old. It's hard to believe that we've been married for over thirty-five years. One day soon, I'll be able to slow down—then we can do all the things we've missed."

"As for today," I continued, "we finish taping at nine. Then I'll go direct to the airport to catch a one-thirty flight to Orlando. I have three shows to do there with Clay Hart and Salli Flynn. From there, I'll go on to join the band in Tucson, Dallas, Knoxville, Gainesville, West Palm Beach, Lakeland, St. Pete, Fort Myers, Biloxi, and Austin. I'll be home on March 8 about ten-forty in the evening. I'll have missed your birthday by only one day this year."

"I'm getting used to *that* after all these years, but time doesn't make it any easier! Want some breakfast before you leave?"

Later, as I'm polishing off a bowl of cereal laced with bananas and low-fat milk, two basted eggs, bacon, and a cup of coffee, Berdyne says, "Even after all these years, I can't see how you can eat with such relish just after you get up in the morning."

"Honey," I answer, "that's what we did back on the farm. And, as you know, you can take the boy off the farm, but you can't take the farm out of the boy. Oh, Oh! It's eight forty-five. Time to head for the studio."

"The story of my life," she replies sadly. "Saying good-bye and 'I'll see you later.' Well, try to have a safe trip."

Most of my life consists of making deadlines for shows, airplanes, rehearsals, and appointments. I live by the calendar and clock. Even so, I feel no stress from all this activity. I guess I even thrive on it. All the hustle and bustle is probably the reason that I'm alive and healthy today. For a while, I thought of naming this book *The Wandering Minstrel!*

As the car warms up, I check my supplies for the next eleven days. Let's see now...two accordions, a box of music for the shows, my aluminum suitcase (a very practical gift from the band on my twenty-fifth anniversary with them), three uniforms, briefcase with all my "homework" and contracts, U.S. atlas and official airline guide (referred to as the OAG by seasoned travelers, it's issued every two weeks so we can keep up with the constantly changing airline schedules). Finally I check my billfold—never more than $100 in cash, credit cards, and VIP cards for the special airline waiting rooms.

Back in 1950 we were on the road for months at a time. Without wash-and-wear clothes, I wonder how we ever managed to get by; we must have been pretty gamy at times. I surely don't envy the members of road bands in the thirties and forties. They traveled by bus day after day, sometimes doing "jumps" (the distance between jobs) of three to five hundred miles at a time. Luckily for all of us, the Musicians Union finally established a three-hundred-mile limit for daily travel between jobs.

I pull out of the driveway and head for ABC studios, thirty-four miles away, at Prospect and Talmadge in Hollywood. The drive, which will take about fifty minutes, includes twenty-two miles on the freeways and about twelve miles on surface roads. I know that there are forty-eight stoplights on my way—every morning I pray that I'll make all the green lights!

Driving onto the ABC parking lot, I'm reminded of our early days at the studio. The place is full of history. Part of Al Jolson's movie *The Jazz Singer* was filmed here, along with *A Night at the Opera* starring the Marx Brothers. I can almost hear Al Jolson singing "Mammy" on the stage

170

as the Marx Brothers upstage him by creating mayhem wherever they go.

I remember walking into the studio for our first day's filming. I overheard one of the stage hands ask the head prop man, "How long should we check these scenery flats our for?"

"Oh, just for a few days," came the answer. "This bunch won't last long! I just can't see a band doing a show without a comedian or even a line of dancing girls. Nobody will watch! I'll bet they won't last three weeks!"

Well, it's been nearly thirty years. I hope that guy didn't bet much on our demise!

As I carry my two accordions, music case, and uniforms into the studio that day in February, I reflect on the active life I've led. Maybe a bit too busy these past few years: 170 dates in 1980 alone! I really should think of slowing down some. After all, Berdyne has waited patiently long enough for those "good times" I promised her. I'm finally beginning to realize that the nice house, cars, and other "goodies" aren't really what a woman wants out of life. The really important thing is time together. I've just got to give her more of that. She's right—we're not getting any younger.

God has given me more chances than I deserve already. After all, five years ago I almost went down for the count.

September 14, 1975. York, Pennsylvania. My accordion seemed to weigh a thousand pounds as I stumbled into my hotel room. I was drenched in sweat and feeling very nauseated.

"Just over-tired," I thought to myself. "This ugly feeling will pass just as soon as I've had a good shower and some sleep."

I undressed quickly and let the hot water in the shower fill the bathroom with steam. As I stepped into the shower, I was hit by violent chills. The hot water just seemed to aggravate my miserable feeling. I couldn't stop shaking. I dried off and got an extra blanket from the closet. Even in bed with an extra cover, I couldn't relax and get warm. The chills actually felt even worse.

"Maybe just a touch of the flu?" I wondered as I lay there reviewing the past couple of weeks to figure where I might have picked up a bug like this.

I had just finished a Lawrence Welk tour that took me to sixteen different cities in sixteen days. We had done only one show a day plus the travel time...really about average as our tours went. I shouldn't have been so tired after that trip.

Finally, I willed myself to sleep. I just *knew* that if I could rest for at least one night, I would be rid of whatever was making me feel so sick.

As I look back, I wonder how I could have been so wrong!

The next morning I *did* feel a lot better, and figured that I probably had just been struck by one of those twenty-four-hour viruses. But as each day passed, I became weaker. Every job became a terrible chore, and finally even *I* had to admit that something was very wrong.

At Berdyne's urging I made an appointment with Dr. Hackie for a thorough checkup.

"It looks like a bad case of the flu, Myron," Dr. Hackie said. "But I want you to have a couple lab tests to rule out SBE."

SBE? I didn't quite have the nerve to ask what that was. Dr. Hackie sounded so serious that I was very relieved when the tests came back negative.

Over a month had passed since that miserable night in York. I continued doing the TV shows and all my outside engagements, but I still felt sick and very tired. What really began to worry my family was that I had almost completely lost my appetite. After all, my girls had grown up watching Daddy eat everything in sight! Now even Berdyne's special cooking failed to tempt me, and I had lost nearly twenty pounds.

My hearing began to seem muffled; sounds reached me as though they were coming from very far away. I kept on with all my jobs, including one in Lincoln, Nebraska, where I worked with Bobby Layne, the local orchestra leader. Bobby traveled in a motor home that I was able to sleep in between each show. That was all that kept me going!

By November, I could hardly get around. I just kept thinking of December, when I had a few days off and could just rest. Meanwhile I had my eighth annual week in New Braunfels, Texas, to look forward to. Ordinarily, their *Wurstfest* (sausage festival) is my favorite date of the whole year. Berdyne always joins me there, and those wonderful Texas Germans really show us a good time. This year, however, I dreaded the trip. I knew that my illness would never allow me to give the audience what they deserved, and I couldn't bear the idea of disappointing them.

Tom Purdum, of the Chamber of Commerce and of the festival, met Berdyne and me at the San Antonio airport. His usual happy greeting was cut short.

"What in the world is wrong with you? You look half dead!" he said.

"Just a touch of the flu," I answered as convincingly as I could.

"We hope!" Berdyne added. "I'm not so sure, and I'd like him to see Dr. Stanley Woodward while we're here."

"No problem," Tom answered. "I'll drive you both over to his office in the morning!"

My first show was set for seven-thirty that evening. As showtime neared, the weakness and nausea hit me again. I couldn't remember what songs I had decided to do. When I finally headed for the stage, surrounded by security guards, I felt like I could probably handle about fifteen minutes, far less than half of my usual show length.

Then I was on stage, and that love flowing from the audience seemed to give me more strength than I had been able to muster in weeks. I forgot my discomfort and fatigue and did the entire hour-long show. At the end of the hour, though, there was very little left of me. I felt as if I had melted away into a huge puddle of sweat. The second show that evening? I don't even remember it.

"I think you should go directly to the DeBakey Institute in Houston. You're in deep trouble." Dr. Woodward, like Dr. Hackie, didn't pull any punches. He had just finished a thorough examination and was looking at my X-rays.

"But they specialize in heart surgery!" I protested. "I'd have to cancel an awful lot of jobs!"

"I hate to be so blunt," Dr. Woodward continued. "But if you don't get this taken care of very soon, you won't be doing any jobs. You'll be dead."

Well, I guess I am a stubborn Norwegian. Sometimes a house has to fall on me before I pay attention!

"Okay, Doc," I said finally, "I'll finish the Wurstfest and a couple more jobs and then on our Christmas break I'll check into a hospital in Los Angeles."

"I hope you make it that far!" he said ominously.

By Thanksgiving I could no longer pretend that time would end my problems. I made one more call to Dr. Hackie.

"Get another test done for SBE," he said. "And don't wait. This is serious!"

I got out our medical encyclopedia. There I found the answer I had been trying so hard not to hear: "Subacute Bacterial Endocarditis...a strep infection of the lining of the heart...always fatal."

Fatal! That word was the last brick of the house falling on my head. I ran out the door and headed for the nearest hospital. They took several blood samples and said they would call me. That evening I was scheduled to play at a retirement village near Long Beach. Bob and Kristie came along and carried the show for me. I'm not even *sure* what I did. The next morning I checked into St. Vincent's Hospital in Los Angeles.

After what seemed like hundreds of blood tests, X-rays, and other tests I can't even remember, Drs. Jerome Kay and Bernard Krohn came in to talk with Berdyne and me.

"Mr. Floren, you do have SBE. It's been present for quite a long time, and we can't tell just yet how much damage it's done. We want to put you on intravenous penicillin to get rid of the strep germ that's causing the infection; then after you've had time to rest and regain some of your strength, we'll have to perform open heart surgery. If it's any consolation, SBE is no longer always fatal; penicillin has been used against it with a lot of success."

"Dr. Krohn," I said, "I'm allergic to penicillin."

"Well, it's the only drug available—but there are lots of derivatives. We'll just keep trying till one of them works."

That afternoon I began receiving massive doses of medication through a needle in my left arm. By morning the arm was discolored and swollen to almost twice its normal size. A couple of other drugs were tried with the same results. By the third day, I was really low. Nothing seemed to work against the germ.

Then Dr. Krohn told me he had decided to try a new drug that had just become available—Keflex. I was more than ready for a miracle and began to pray with all the strength I had left.

The Keflex worked!

For the next four weeks I received the Keflex four times each day. Gradually I began to feel like my old self again. After the second week in the hospital, Berdyne began bringing in the cards and letters that had come in the mail wishing me a speedy recovery. I had forgotten how much I missed being out on the job, and those wishes from so many friends made me more determined to get well quickly and get back to work. But I still had to face surgery—that I knew.

All of my show and dance jobs had to be canceled, of course. Dick Dale, Jack Imel, Gail Farrell, and others from the band stood in for me at many of the dates as far ahead as March. Most of the booking agents and promoters were very understanding...but there was one who wanted me just to show up in a wheelchair to prove I was really sick!

About a week before Christmas, Berdyne and I were talking quietly when we heard a big commotion out in the hallway. We were just beginning to wonder what was going on, when in walked Tanya and Larry Welk, Guy and Ralna Hovis, and Clay and Salli Hart. They were dragging a Christmas tree and boxes full of ornaments and decorations, which they proceeded to put up all over the room! As they trimmed the little tree we all visited and joked, until when they finally left, wishing us a Merry Christmas, I was too emotional to say good-bye. I thanked God for all my wonderful family and friends who mean so much to me.

On Christmas Day, Berdyne and all my girls plus Bob Burgess, Albena, and Art gathered around my hospital bed for Christmas morning before they went on to a family party at Betty and Ken's home. They handed out gifts and love, and when they left at about two in the afternoon, I was hooked up to my intravenous medicine again. I fell asleep almost immediately and began to dream.

I walked through that same forest I had gone through as a child with rheumatic fever. This time there was no fierce dog, and when I reached the edge of the woods, I heard a voice from the light: "Not yet. You have more to do." I knew I was dreaming, and I settled into the most restful sleep I had had in months.

The following morning I knew that I was on my way back to health. Even my breakfast cornflakes tasted good! When Dr. Krohn came in he had even better news for me—the latest blood tests showed that the infection was nearly cleared up. Now, he said, they could begin to prepare me for heart surgery. Good news and bad news!

During the next few days I took a treadmill test and many others designed to evaluate the health and strength of my heart. Dr. Krohn really had good news for me then. No heart surgery would be needed! By some miracle, my heart had healed enough so, at least for the time being, I did not have to face surgery.

The doctors commented that the work of playing the accordion had kept my body so strong that I probably would never die from heart problems. "Your veins and arteries are like wide freeways," they said. Now, that gave me a start, as I envisioned the Los Angeles freeway during the morning and afternoon rush.

I was released from the hospital on New Year's Eve with instructions to take it easy for a few weeks, then go back to my old schedule—only make it a little lighter from now on. Six weeks later, I was back in full swing again.

In 1979, I visited Dr. Krohn for a checkup. After all the tests he asked me, "How do you feel?"

"Like a million dollars, Doc," I answered.

"Your heart murmur has almost disappeared," he said. "By the way, did I tell you that Keflex had become available only three weeks before you entered the hospital?"

And I thought Lawrence Welk had the corner on good timing!

Four Special People

I believe very strongly that God wants my musical career to be a ministry of music for Him. I feel that this is why I have been spared during serious illnesses, and why my interests were eventually guided to and centered on music. So whenever I play for entertainment or for special occasions, I feel an obligation to bring joy, peace, and comfort to those who hear me. This is the way in which I carry out the will of God to serve my fellow men while serving Him.

There are many others who are similarly serving, but in their own, individual ways. Some, just with their concern and faith, dispense comfort and joy. I often find myself the recipient of their desire to serve God, and my life is influenced and improved. My bread is returned with butter.

There is an old hymn that says, "God moves in a mysterious way His wonders to perform." I believe this, even though at times I find it difficult to understand why a person may have to go through pain and suffering to fulfill his mission. But that is without doubt one of the "mysterious ways" in which God works, and who am I to question?

I have been the recipient of great good and of God's love bestowed upon me by many people, but by four in

179

particular. And I believe as sincerely as I believe anything that each one of them, with his own talents, was put here for a divine purpose and was fulfilling the will of God. One was my mother, one was my sister Gloria, one was my father, and the other was a lovely lady named Doris Tirrell.

Let me tell you about them.

GLORIA

Gloria, my youngest sister, was eight years old when I left Webster to attend Augustana. I didn't know it then, but I would see her very little during the rest of her life. She would have been about twelve or thirteen when my whole family moved to Sioux Falls about nineteen forty. At the time, I was busy with college and broadcasting and generally would leave the house in the morning before the younger ones were up. With my busy schedule coupled with the tour of Europe with USO and then the move to St. Louis, it was hard for me to notice how quickly my sisters and brother Duane were growing up.

All of a sudden I discovered she was a grown woman, getting married to Herb Peterson. And before I knew it, although it couldn't have happened too fast, she had a son and two daughters, and we got an announcement that another daughter was born. We sent our congratulations.

About a year later, we were living in Windsor Hills, and a letter from my sister Genevieve arrived. It was September, and I often thought about the trees back home in South Dakota, changing into their beautiful fall colors; a beautiful time of year, but...

Doctors had discovered a lump in one of her breasts.

180

All those years I'd missed out seeing her and the rest of the family. No way to make up that time. I was afraid my little sister was going to die, and I'd hardly known her. Berdyne tried to console me, but I knew the terrible truth—cancer. And in a young, active person, I understood that it spread more rapidly.

I wrote a letter, but how could I cover all those years of neglect? Her answer came back. She was going to Rochester to the Mayo Clinic for an operation to remove the cancerous breast. I talked to the doctors after the surgery. They were sure they had gotten all of the malignant cells. I breathed easier, still not convinced.

Thanksgiving came and then Christmas, with no apparent change in her condition. I was scheduled to participate in Roslyn's 75th anniversary program in May. I eagerly anticipated seeing Gloria, hoping she was recovering. I wasn't prepared for the mob of people in Roslyn. I arrived just in time to ride in the parade with Dad and Mother. After the parade I did a couple of shows. Gloria's arm was not in a sling, but she held it strangely and stiffly. When I asked her quietly how she was, she said, "Not too bad. It seems to be getting better."

I said, "We'll see you at home tomorrow when there aren't so many people around." I went mechanically through the shows and the rest of the day. Dad and Mother, too, showed their concern, but hid it well from everyone at the celebration.

The next morning from the folks' little home north of Sioux Falls, I called Gloria's doctor, Stanley Devick, a classmate of mine from Augustana. "Stanley," I said, "What's the truth about Gloria's condition?"

"Myron, I'm terribly sorry. She has a rare kind of cancer that acts very swiftly. She has a month—maybe three months at the most." Again: "I'm sorry."

"There's nothing any of us can do?" I choked out.

"Nothing. She's a wonderful patient and is facing her passing more bravely than anyone I know. But there's no hope."

She and Herb and the kids came over in the afternoon, and we visited. Where she had been lively, happy, and carefree the last time I had seen her, she was quiet, quite thin, and more beautiful than I ever remembered.

"I don't know why I should be the one to go first of our family," she said soberly. "But evidently God has a plan for me and for all of us. I can't understand it now, but I'm sure that someday I will. I feel sorry for Herb and my kids, but in time they'll get over it." Then: "You shouldn't work so hard, Myron. It's bad for your health." Bad for *my* health.

She managed to be happy and smiling around the kids and had even brought her special Angel Salad—her own recipe—for our lunch that afternoon. We ate and tried to talk of less serious things, I talking of my upcoming jobs with Lawrence Welk, and Herb and Gloria telling of their plans for later in the summer. I was glad that they had paid us a visit in California a few years before.

When they left that afternoon, Gloria held her newest baby as Herb swung the car around. That last picture of Gloria alive is etched into my memory. I knew I might never see her again.

I was on the stage at Harrah's at Lake Tahoe during the middle of July. The packed houses for each show applauded loudly and long after each number. But all of a sudden I would feel like crying. Thoughts of Gloria were uppermost in my mind. We had had no deaths in the family. Maybe there was still some magic cure. I called her every day from Tahoe. Lawrence and the band sent birthday cards July 6, and she was most appreciative, especially with the card from Lawrence.

Halfway through the appearance we learned she was back in the hospital suffering from jaundice and swelling all over her body. The doctor said it was only a matter of days—maybe a week.

Berdyne, the girls, and I returned to our home in Windsor Hills, and I called the hospital. Her voice was as strong as ever, even though I knew she must be going down rapidly.

I played for the American Guild of Music in Kentucky on Wednesday. On Thursday I played a fair in Orange County. Friday I placed my usual call to Gloria at Sioux Valley Hospital. The nurse, her voice choking, handed the phone to a doctor. "I'm sorry, Myron. Gloria is not here."

"You mean she has gone home?"

"Mrs. Peterson expired about an hour ago."

I handed the phone to Berdyne, unable to speak. Berdyne spoke to the doctor. Services would probably be Monday. I stumbled out of the room. Kristie met me. "I'm sorry, Dad," she said, hugging me, and two big tears running down her cheeks. I had said the same thing to my dad when his father passed away a generation earlier.

Gloria's funeral was large. She had been very popular, drawing people to her with her sunny disposition and abiding faith in God. She had been a good neighbor.

The family minister had been deeply impressed with the way she approached death. "She had no fear—just faith that death was not the end but a new beginning, where all of God's wonders would finally be clear to her." Faith that we should, "rest assured, we will meet again—with God."

I was hit hard by regret. Why hadn't I written more frequently? Why couldn't we have gotten together more?

We all fall into the trap of thinking we have many years ahead of us, plenty of time to write or call or visit; so we put it off. But death has a habit of surprising us. It can strike in an instant—a crashing airplane, a car out of control, a slip in a bathtub—or come quietly as the proverbial thief in the night. We are never ready.

A few months later, driving across Iowa about four in the morning, I dozed at the wheel. As my car headed for a steep ditch, Gloria's voice shouted, "Wake up, Myron!" I stopped short of the ditch. When I stopped shaking, I noticed a small white cloud momentarily shut out the light of a bright full moon.

"Thank you, Gloria."

DAD

During the days we were home for Gloria's funeral, I noticed Dad from time to time doubled over as if in great pain. When questioned, he would say, "It's just a stomachache." But he promised to see a doctor if he didn't improve. When we left for California, he said he was better, but from the tone of his voice, we weren't so sure. We knew that Gloria's death had been a great shock, and maybe that was part of the reason he was feeling poorly.

We called often during the next couple of months. Still pain. Then a letter from Mother. Dad was to go into the hospital for an operation to find, if possible, the cause of his discomfort.

Berdyne was with me in Pueblo, Colorado, where I was playing the state fair, when a letter came. Surgery would be performed the next day.

We called about noon. The verdict made me feel again the hopeless anger that something was happening to one of my loved ones, and I was powerless to do anything about it.

There was no cure. Only a matter of time. But how much? Maybe a month—maybe three months. Our family had been indestructible, and yet here in the space of three months it looked as if we were being decimated.

We returned to Los Angeles, but the following week I was booked for two days to play the fair in Oshkosh, Wisconsin, with Brenda Lee. After that I would fly to Sioux Falls to see Dad. But before leaving, I wrote to him:

Dear Dad:

In our busy lives how many of us tend to postpone thanking those special ones we love the most for the help and inspiration they have been in our lives. I hope I have shown you and Mother how much I appreciate the faith you have had in me. Whatever measure of success I have attained can be credited to you because of your early and continued support and love. Berdyne, Randee, Kristie, Robin, Holly and Heidi all send their love and prayers. God bless you.

Your loving son,
Myron

After autographing and shaking hands at the first show, I placed a call to Mother. Dad was back in the hospital. He'd taken a sudden turn for the worse.

I chartered a plane to Sioux Falls the next morning. We left Oshkosh at six. Weather was bad, and we fought headwinds all across Wisconsin. Weather reports predicted a storm later in the day over the entire area. Our arrival was an hour and a half late.

Then, before going to the hospital, I rented a car and drove hurriedly to my folks' home north of town to pick up Mother and Valborg, who had returned to help. As we were

185

hurrying out the door, the phone rang. Valborg answered it, then said nothing, but handed the receiver to Mother. Mother listened for a moment, murmured, "Thank you," and slowly hung up the phone. "Dad is gone," she said haltingly, and then, pointing to an envelope on the piano, "and he didn't even get to read your letter." And then Mother, the calmest of all, said, "We better get to the hospital. There'll be a lot of details to straighten out."

Mother and Dad were alike in moments of grief. Keep doing something, anything, to keep the mind and heart going. Life still has to go on.

The night before, Pa had had a good visit with Mother, his sister Julia, brother Mike, and my cousin George. He had felt fine and told jokes with the rest of them.

"Well, Ole," Julia finally said, "Visiting hours are over and you better get some sleep. You know Myron is coming in the morning."

"Yes, I know," was his answer. "But I'm not tired. I don't need much sleep tonight. Tomorrow I'm going to sleep for a million years."

Even then they thought Dad was having a little joke.

After making arrangements for the funeral, we returned to the house. The plane I had chartered was waiting to return me to Oshkosh for the second show.

"We didn't make it," I told the pilot. "Let's go."

The storm that had been predicted broke in all its fury as we flew into Wisconsin heading for Oshkosh. We were flying a two-motored Bonanza through rain and hail so heavy it seemed as if there might be yet another death in the family before the day ended. We were fighting a downdraft as well as the deluge of water. I didn't see how the plane could make it. I glanced at the pilot; sweat was pouring from his face. A horn warning us of a stall was

186

shrill in our ears. It was almost as if God were telling me He understood my feelings and wanted me to be near the breaking point before—suddenly we were in brilliant sunshine. No clouds, no rain, no storm, no hail! I thought, "Am I dreaming again? Will I wake up and find this is all a bad dream?"

But it was no dream. Dad was gone. But God, I am sure, sent the storm to let me know that no matter how bad it might be, He was with me—today and always.

I suddenly felt whole again, and my faith in the future and life returned. It was a born-again feeling, much like a good shower of rain on the farm that used to clear the dust and dirt from the air. I breathed deeply. The pilot, noticing the sudden change, said, "Are you all right?"

"I'm fine," I answered. "How soon till we get to Oshkosh?"

"Fifteen minutes—but you know, for a while back there, I thought my number was up."

"I know what you mean," I said. "But everything is going to be fine now. Life has to go on."

The services for Dad were a celebration of his life. No other kind would have been appropriate. Never one to be conquered by problems and misfortune, he always felt there was a new day ahead. Life was to be lived, problems were to be overcome, and with God as his inspiration and constant companion, despair was unknown to him. It was from Dad that I had learned that life must go on.

Later that day we began to reminisce, and recalled many happy times with him:

"Remember the year one of the neighbors shot our dog when we were right there playing with it?" one of us asked. Dad had driven over to the neighbors, who hurriedly put their car in the garage. "Been out hunting?" Dad asked. "No," they said, "been home all day." Dad opened the garage door to find the water still boiling in the radiator. We didn't hear what happened, but we never had any trouble from them again.

"Remember the year we had potatoes in the field over the hill from the house?" someone else asked. One morning we had gone out to dig some for dinner and discovered a whole row had been dug up. But the thieves had left a trail. In the Ford we followed the potato trail to a trailer west of our place, picking up potatoes as we went along. When we got there, we found our potatoes all right, but next to the trailer was a group of little ragged gypsy kids, some of them biting into raw potatoes. At first Pa didn't say anything; then he reached in back of the Ford and got out the pailfull we had picked up along the way. "Here's some more. By the way, bring your trailer over; I'll fix that hole in the box."

As we drove away, brother Arlie and I asked, "How come you didn't do anything to them? You know they stole our potatoes."

Again he was silent for a long time. Then finally: "Well, when I saw those little ragged kids eating raw potatoes, I said, 'Lord, thank you for sending those little children to my potato field.' We couldn't let them starve, could we, when we have so much?"

Brother Arlie, tracing a circle in the dust on the dashboard with the big toe that was sticking out of the hole in his shoe said, "Boy, I hope we never get poor."

DORIS

"Am I still a tiger?" Doris asked wistfully.

"Indeed you are!" I choked out.

188

"Do you still think I'll be home for Christmas?"

"Yes, Doris, I feel certain you'll be home then."

Doris Tirrell was one of the thousands of rare people I have met through music. She typified the unconquerable spirit of the people who make up the backbone of the American dream.

Doris lived all her life in the same house in Brockton, Massachusetts. For some reason she never married, but not for lack of suitors, I'm sure.

She was an organist of rare talent and accomplishment, known and loved by all who met her. All who had contact with her—even for an instant—through lessons or in her concerts, felt their lives enriched by the love and compassion of this woman.

My association with Doris Tirrell came about through the powerful medium of TV and some little teaching pieces I had done for Remick Music in New York. "Saucy Miss," a little accordion number that Remick had transcribed for piano, was the catalyst that brought us together. The song could have been written with this dedicated lady in mind. She lived for her hundreds of students and her endless benefits for church and community.

As her friend and musical partner Walter Lendh would say, "She doesn't care about money at all." And this to Walter, who was in the loan department of the Brockton Savings Bank, was hard to understand. He'd shake his head mystified. "She always says the money will come in if it's meant to be."

Walter also played very fine piano and appeared with Doris on most of her shows. He also had the car.

When Doris first wrote to me, it was to say how much the TV show and music meant to her and to find out if there

189

was the remotest possibility of my doing a concert with her and Walter at the Brockton high school. About this time the Lawrence Welk Orchestra was set to play Boston Gardens, and I suggested that she attend and we could discuss the matter. She had impressed me through her letters, but I was totally unprepared for the diminutive bundle of dynamite that was Doris Tirrell. Past 65 years when I met her in the early 1960s, she was going as strong as ever with no thought of retiring or slowing down.

"I've got too many things to do to retire now. The government can't tell me when to go out to pasture," she would say as she peered at me through thick lenses that made her eyes look especially large. I could imagine her students thinking they better get their lessons right, because she would see every wrong move.

Up until 1978 Doris, Walter, and I played well over one hundred benefit concerts in the eastern part of Massachusetts. I became as much at home there as I ever had in South Dakota. We later added David Benjamin from Stoughton as vocalist, and many times made use of high school bands, orchestras, and vocal groups. We weren't the Boston Pops, but the crowds we drew were always warm and special and, I thought, a tribute to a gallant lady and her music.

For the last year or so, Doris had trouble getting around. She would lean on Walter, David, or myself to negotiate unfamiliar steps, but once perched on her organ bench, she was mistress of any situation. We raised money for hospitals, library guilds, Rotary clubs, Lions clubs, school organizations—you name it, we did it. Sometimes a sponsor would call to say tickets weren't moving. Doris wasted no time. The telephone was invented for her. She'd sit down in her kitchen where the phone was within easy

190

reach, and before you could say "Jeremiah Bullfrog," things would be humming. Always toward the end of our concerts we would play "Tiger Rag," and she had a special stop on the organ that would imitate the growl of a tiger. Oftentimes when things weren't going exactly the way she wanted, she would call just to talk. In minutes she'd be her old indestructible self and close by saying, "Well, I feel like a tiger again."

During these days I renewed my friendship with Sandy Rozell, my pal from USO days. He appeared on many of our concerts. His "fish horn" didn't sound as it once did, but the fire was still there. Doris, Walter, and I would play his act, and I would relive for a few minutes our days in Camp Shows. Sandy passed on a few years ago, but I'm sure that his fish horn, combat boots, and kilts are still making someone happy somewhere.

"Hello, this is sick tiger calling." In a voice heavy with care and frustration, Doris called in August 1980.

"I had some dental work done today, and the doctor found a tumor. They want me to go to the hospital to have it looked after. What should I do?"

"Doris," I answered, "I think you better do as the doctors advise. We'll pray that it's something simple."

This time Doris wasn't fooled. When she called back a couple of days later, I could tell by her tone that what she had feared had been diagnosed—cancer in her upper gums and sinuses. She was advised to go to a nursing home where she would have twenty-four-hour care.

"Do you think I'll ever see home again?" she phoned one day.

"I'm sure you will, Doris," I said. "Remember you're a tiger, and you're the kind of tiger that never gives up."

"Guess you're right. Tell everybody 'hello' and that I love them, especially Holly. You know, I've never met that girl, but I feel like I know her so well. We have such a good time communicating with each other." Doris had seen pictures of all my girls but never had or would meet any of them. But through the phone they were old friends.

"Doris," I said, "my schedule is very heavy, but I'm playing for the Shriners at Symphony Hall in Boston in November, and I'll be out to see you."

During the next few weeks, whenever I called Doris, she would be brought to a phone in the office. Her general health was deteriorating rapidly. A week before I was scheduled to be in Boston, I made my usual call. The nurse informed me that Doris was too ill to come to the phone. "I'll be in to see her on Sunday afternoon. Will you tell her that?"

"Yes, and I hope she'll still be here," the nurse answered, a catch in her voice.

When I arrived, the nurse stopped me in the hallway. "Are you sure you want to go in?" she asked. "It's very shocking to see her. We tried to fit her with a mask, but it wouldn't stay on."

"She's expecting me, isn't she?" And to her affirmative reply I said that I must see her.

"Yes, knowing you were coming has kept her spirits up, and she has told everyone in the nursing home you're coming."

"May I play the accordion for her?" I asked, feeling that if I had my accordion, playing it would get me through the shock.

"She'd love that," answered the nurse.

While my accordion was being brought up, the nurse and I walked into her room, but I was not prepared for

192

what I saw. Trying not to betray my feelings, I said, "How's my tiger today?"

"Not too good, but now that you're here, I'm feeling better."

Holding the accordion helped me regain control of myself, and I asked if she had any request. "Play what we used to close the show with—play 'Tiger Rag.'"

I glanced around while playing—flowers everywhere. Here was a fighter whose friends had not forgotten. There were so many familiar names—Walter, David, and Bettina Kyper of the *Brockton Enterprise,* always a staunch supporter of Doris over the years.

And Doris sat bedside, her fingers moving as though on the organ keyboard. I hit a wrong note in the bass, and she corrected me: "Wrong note there; should be F-sharp."

Even in their failing health, other patients joined us, some clapping to the music, others singing while a couple of nurses danced about. Again, music was the common bond where all could share happier memories and for a few moments be at peace. The smiles, requests, and the sound of voices singing were my great reward.

As I finished my impromptu performance, which had now stretched into over an hour, the nurse said, "You'll never know how much this has meant to her."

"I think I do," I replied. "Maybe a small part of what it has meant to me."

As I bent to kiss her forehead, Doris asked again, "Am I still a tiger?"

And I replied, "Indeed you are!"

"Do you still think I'll be home for Christmas?"

"Yes, Doris, I feel certain you'll be home then."

She went to her permanent home eight days before the holidays.

MOM

Bob Johnson, my brother-in-law, married to my sister Genevieve, called from McKennan Hospital in Sioux Falls a few minutes after midnight New Year's Day in nineteen seventy-eight.

His voice was quiet. "Tillie passed away just a few minutes ago. She just went to sleep."

Mother was past eighty when she was called to her Maker.

After the funeral at the First Lutheran Church in Sioux Falls all of us Floren children reminisced about our mother. Her quiet strength through good times and bad was one of her great virtues.

Her happiness came from doing good for others. Most of her work when we were growing up on the farm was dedicated to doing things that would make life a little more pleasant for her seven children and her husband. Her week was a never-ending round of chores. Washing clothes for nine people consumed all of one day but at the same time bread dough would be rising. As she heated water for the washing on the kitchen stove it would be shameful not to use the heat for baking bread, buns, or a cake. Her angel food cake was always a winner and eating the fresh bread hot from the oven with strawberry jam or peanut butter was a treat to be savored and remembered.

The clothesline in our yard was hardly ever empty. The sun and wind were our dryers. If the weather was freezing cold there would be times when the wet shirts and overalls would assume grotesque shapes on the line and we would stack the brittle shirts, diapers, and underwear like so many boards to carry into the house where the drying process would take hours and hours. Even though clothes dryers were available later in her life she pre-

194

ferred the natural way; and the fresh, clean smell of clothes dried in the wind and sun had a scent equal to the most expensive perfume.

Her sewing machine was always busy. When her children moved away from home the sewing machine was even busier making aprons for sale in her church works or putting together patchwork quilts. Her crocheting, quilt making, and sewing extended her quiet love for others in the color and warmth of the things she made. On the farm I remember many of the quilting bees where some of her sisters would come in from nearby towns to help with the tying of the quilts. These quilting days took on the air of a holiday with the conversation and laughter of Ma and her helpers.

Every Sunday after church we would head for Pickerel Lake or a neighboring grove of trees where we could have picnics with a few relatives or friends or sometimes a large gathering like the Fourth of July or *Syttende mai.* Opening the picnic baskets was always a thrill for us brothers and sisters. Ma's cooking was always special.

To the day she died Ma was busy with plans for more afghans and aprons. I like to think that in her new life she is making her presence felt with showing others how to make a dress, bake a better loaf of bread, or sew on a patch, all in her quiet unassuming way.

I was honored in 1978 and 1979 by being asked to serve as the national co-chairman of the American Cancer Society with Amanda Blake. The four special people I have mentioned gave me a personal involvement. Some day a cure will be found. It won't be able to bring back any of our loved ones but their influence on the lives that continue is strong and ever binding.

The Champagne
Music Makers

I arrive at the studio on February 25, 1981, with fifteen
minutes to spare before we begin our day's work on the last
show of the year. I unpack my accordion, music, and program schedule, and place them on the stand. Then I head
for the coffee urn, where I meet Lawrence already pouring
hot water for his morning cup of tea.

"Ready for another good show?" he asks.

"Sure am," I answer. "Not just for another show, but
for another good year! You look like you're ready, too."

"Yes," he says. "Aren't we lucky?! We have good
health, our viewers, our band, and all the wonderful
people associated with us. Did you ever think back on the
farm that life would turn out so great?"

"Well," I reply, "I always did have some pretty big
plans, but in my wildest dreams I never imagined things
would be so great as they've been since I joined "Champagne Music"; now I feel that we still have lots of good
years ahead of us."

With my coffee in hand, I turn to the band members
already in their places. Barney Liddell, our bass trombone
man, and Curt Ramsey, our band librarian, are talking
about Larry Hooper. Larry has been out ill for most of the

197

last twelve months. He's had open heart surgery twice, and several heart attacks, but he has always managed to keep his sense of humor intact. Joining them, I share a story about our early travels with Larry.

We were driving across Iowa, and we decided to stop and stretch. "Hoopy" got out of the bus and stood by the fenced pasture, giving out loud hog calls. Soon we were surrounded by about a hundred pigs...all very anxious to see where those sexy sounds were coming from!

Larry has often said he never would have survived those illnesses if it hadn't been for the love of his wife, Beverly, and all the prayers offered by his thousands of fans.

Barney, Dick Dale, George Cates, and Curt are all members of what I like to call our thirty-year club. We have all been with Lawrence for over thirty years—and I think I speak for all of us when I say we hope for another thirty!

Barney joined the band two years before me, so he is the senior member. He comes from Gary, Indiana, and was with the Teddy Phillips band originally. At first he wasn't sure he could stand playing with such a "square" band, but after thirty-two years, I think he must have decided that he likes it after all!

Barney handles all the transportation of our instruments, costumes, and props when we go on the road. He drives the truck to and from the airports, or, if the distance between appearances is less than two hundred miles, he drives the truck there himself. Either way, our trips are made much easier because of all his hard work.

Our producer walks into the production area where our "boys and girls" are gathered for a rehearsal of Irving Berlin's "Easter Parade." Jim Hobson has been with us

198

since our first show at ABC in 1955. He started out in TV as a cameraman for the "Liberace Show." With him are Jim Roberts, who joined us in 1954, and his singing partner, Norma Zimmer. Norma is a gracious lady and has been our very fine Champagne Lady since 1960. Through the years, their duets have been very popular; they are also outstanding soloists.

"One minute to rehearsal," I hear Irving Ross announce over the loudspeaker. Our timing schedule rivals the Cape Canaveral launchings! The last ten seconds are counted down by the floor director, and precisely at ten o'clock, George Cates gives the downbeat for the fanfare to open the show. Lawrence always enters at center stage to make his first announcement, and we are "launched" into our show for the week.

The members of the 1981 Champagne Music Makers could make up a "mini" United Nations, and I believe that variety is the biggest reason for our success. We've always had something for everyone. As different as we all are—in age, religion, or social background—music is our common bond. We are all dedicated musicians, ready to give up almost everything to pursue our craft. Our "time in service" varies from thirty-two to two years, and we have learned to take advantage of that "generation" gap to improve our shows. Our thirty years on television stands as a monument to our success.

Norma and Jim are the charter members of our twenty-year club. Others with about that much time include Gus Thow, Jack Imel, Joe Feeney, Harry Hyams, Bob Havens, Russ Klein, Bob Burgess, Kenny Trimble, and Neal LeVang.

Gus Thow started out as a dixieland-style trumpet player, but Lawrence noted that he was a Harvard man and steered him toward writing instead. Today nearly all the announcements you hear on our TV show are written by Gus.

Jack Imel came to us from the Horace Heidt Show, where his specialties were the marimba, tap dancing, and the drums. Now he is a valued member of our production staff, and his weekly novelty numbers with Mary Lou Metzger are among the highlights of our show.

Jack is full of stories from his days with Horace Heidt. Here's one of my favorites:

Mr. Heidt had an idea for a bit where his whole band would juggle tennis balls. For weeks all the musicians worked to perfect the techniques. Finally the big moment arrived in a famous New York theater. The band went into its juggling routine right on cue, but suddenly tennis balls were bouncing and rolling all over the stage. They had rehearsed without spotlights, and when the lights were turned on, everyone was blinded just long enough for the balls to go astray! The crowd loved it!

Bob Havens came to us in 1960 from Quincy, Illinois, by way of New Orleans, where he was a featured member of the Al Hirt band. Even after twenty-one years, I'm still amazed by his virtuosity. No one can improvise like he does! When Bob first joined us, his act included a number in which he would lie on his back and play his trombone with his foot. He stopped that, though, when he got a huge sliver of wood caught in his backside on an overused stage!

Bob Burgess had been one of Walt Disney's Mouseketeers when he entered our group in 1961. He's had three partners over the years: Barbara Boylan, Cissy King, and Elaine Niverson; all of them have been great assets to our group.

Neal LeVang, our fine guitar man, was born in Adams, North Dakota, and joined us in Seattle. He was well known there as Fiddlin' Neal and had his own local TV show. Neal's background is Swedish—and mine, of course, is Norwegian. But we get along fine in spite of anything you may have heard about the rivalry between Swedes and Norskies.

Our fifteen-year club takes in Bob Ralston (1963), Charlie Parlato (1962), Joe Livoti (1962), Arthur Duncan (1964), and Bob Davis, Don Staples, and Mickey McMahan (all 1960).

Bob Ralston was with Freddy Martin when Lawrence found him. All our fans know what a tremendous pianist Bob is, but they'd be very surprised to find out that he's also a terrific "eccentric" dancer.

Charlie Parlato joined us from the Tennessee Ernie Ford Show. He's a multitalented performer, accomplished at both singing and playing the trumpet. His antics with our dixieland quartet never fail to break me up.

Joe Livoti, our first violinist, is a graduate of the Boston Conservatory, and he can be heard practicing for hours when he has a solo on the show. I've never seen anyone more devoted to music.

Arthur Duncan had just returned from a tour of Australia when one of Lawrence's long-time friends introduced him to us. Arthur had appeared with many of the greats of show business. And he's become one of the most popular members of our group.

Members of the ten-year club include Guy and Ralna Hovis, Mary Lou Metzger, Johnny Zell, Bob Smale, and Gail Farrell.

Ralna was singing at The Horn, a popular Santa Monica club, when Lawrence "discovered" her. Not long after she joined us, he invited her husband, Guy, to appear on the Christmas show. They were so well received that Lawrence decided to keep them as a permanent team.

Today they are extremely popular and very busy with their appearances all over the country.

We were on tour in Phoenix when Lon Varnell asked Lawrence to include Ralna singing "How Great Thou Art" in the show. We had not brought the music along, so I phoned my daughter Kristie and had her dictate the arrangement to me. With the newly copied music in hand, we added the number to the program and received one of the longest standing ovations ever. It's now a permanent part of Ralna's repertoire, and one of her most-requested numbers.

Cute little Mary Lou Metzger came to us from Philadelphia in 1970. Her lively personality has been a great asset in recent years. A lot of people ask me why Lawrence always dances with her at the end of the show... well, I'd dance with her, but since Lawrence is the boss, he gets first chance!

Gail Farrell added her beautiful voice to our show in 1969. She has appeared with me on many personal-appearance tours, and recently we've begun to appreciate her talents on the honky-tonk piano as well. Just this past year, Gail has been joined by her husband, Ron Anderson, and their friend Michael Redman. They've formed a trio with a style very reminiscent of the Pied Pipers and the Modernaires. Gail has also done several vocal arrangements on some of my more-recent albums.

In our five-year-plus club we have Bob Ballard (1973), Ava Barber (1974), Kathi Sullivan (1976), Henry Cuesta (1972), Tom Netherton (1973), Paul Humphrey (1976), and Anacani (1972).

Bob Ballard is one of the finest music arrangers I know. He was associated with us early in our TV career and since 1973 has been a permanent member of the Champagne Music Makers. Our band's rich sound today is

202

largely the result of Bob's work. His arrangements for the Freddy Martin Band and Ray Coniff have become industry standards. Bob did some things for me back in the fifties that are still fresh today.

Ava Barber of Knoxville showed up in 1974. She has become well known in the folk music field and has had a few records on the charts. A beautiful person. Her husband, Roger Sullivan, is a fine drummer.

Kathi Sullivan (no relation to Roger) was guest Champagne Lady in an appearance in Madison, Wisconsin, in 1976. She met Lawrence at the airport to escort him on some TV and talk shows the day we arrived. By the time we left, she was a member of the Champagne Music Makers. A perfect lady on our show, she also has a fine sense of humor and in many personal appearances gets a lot of laughs with her antics.

Henry Cuesta joined us at Harrah's Club at Tahoe in 1972. A finished musician, playing both classical, pop, and jazz on the clarinet and saxophone, Henry always impresses people with his genial personality.

I first met Tom Netherton at the Ramada Inn in Fargo, North Dakota, in 1973. Frank Scott and I were doing a show for Concordia College. We were approached by Tom, who said he would like to sing for us with the idea of getting on the "Lawrence Welk Show." Of course, I didn't need lightning to strike to tell me that here was a man who could really set ladies' hearts thumping. Knowing that Lawrence might not take a recommendation from one of his musicians, I told Tom to get someone in North Dakota to write on his behalf. I found out that he had been appearing at Medora, North Dakota, in a musical play, and must know how to sing. Since Harold Shaffer was the guiding light behind the theater at Medora and I knew that Harold and Lawrence were very close, I suggested that Harold write to Lawrence. Well, a few months later, Tom became a member of our "club." I don't have to go over again the impact he had on our female audience. He is a born-again Christian and is a living testimonial to his clean life and work.

Johnny Klein, our drummer from about 1952 to 1976, is a second cousin of Lawrence Welk. From Strasburg, North Dakota, as well as Lawrence, Johnny was and is a fantastic drummer. By 1976 he had developed a painful ulcer and decided to retire from the band.

To take Johnny's place we were lucky to get Paul Humphrey, a name already well known in jazz and modern music circles. Paul has added his own brand of rhythm to our band. A very dedicated musician.

Anacani, our little Mexican señorita—as Lawrence would say until she married a couple of years ago, ran into Lawrence accidentally at his Mobile Home Park Restaurant in 1972. Lawrence, struck immediately by the beauty of this young lady, asked impulsively, "Are you a movie star?"

"No," Anacani came back. "But I sing."

The magic words. The fact that Anacani sang only in Spanish didn't bother Lawrence. Anacani was added to our family.

Lawrence has for years advocated more training for young people. He has his own program for developing new talent for the show. With us, young people are thrown in with professional musicians and entertainers from their first day. They are able to get the benefit of our years of experience—experience gained from years of hard knocks.

A few years ago we played Nashville. After the show we noticed two very pretty girls waiting for Lawrence backstage. When they finally met Lawrence, he said, after listening to them sing, "If you're on the Coast some-

204

time, stop in to see me." Well, we were due back at about eleven the next morning. Lawrence had to stop by his office to take care of some business. Who should be waiting to see him: the two sisters from Nashville. The Aldridge sisters. As one, Sheila and Sherry spoke up: "Well, you said to look you up if we ever came to California, and here we are!"

"Well, I didn't expect you so soon, but I guess we can find something for you."

The Otwell twins, Roger and David from Tulia, Texas, were suggested by the folks in Tulia. They are becoming more and more popular and their work with the Aldridge sisters is a high spot of our show.

Jim Turner of Knoxville was added in 1979, and his musical stylings with just guitar have become very popular.

Dave Edwards, who played first alto sax with us for years, decided to try the casual field in 1979. So Skeets Herfurt was talked into coming out of retirement to play with us. Skeets's name might not have been too well known to the general public, but his history is long and impressive. Skeets's fine alto has been heard with Glenn Miller, Tommy and Jimmy Dorsey, the Kraft Music Hall, and on and on. We're so happy to have Skeets with us.

When Charlotte Harris, a talented cellist, left us a few years back, Ernie Earhardt took her place. Charlotte had become very popular with our viewers but finally decided a home was more important than a career.

Bobby Burgess joined us in 1960; his partner was Barbara Boylan. Bobby and Barbara added excitement to the show, besides being fresh, young faces. After nine years, Barbara decided that she really wanted a home instead of a career and settled down about 1969. Cissy King came along and the new act was Bobby and Cissy.

Cissy left us in 1979, and Bobby's new partner is Elaine Niverson from Dallas. Each partner has brought new dimensions to our productions and seems to stimulate new interest.

Joey Schmidt, a young accordionist from Napoleon, North Dakota, is our newest addition. We have featured him on many of our shows and have more things lined up for him. I have always enjoyed doing accordion duets, and since Lawrence has let his practicing suffer, Joey and I are having a great time working up new numbers.

I think the rise or fall of any band is the music arrangers. I have mentioned Curt Ramsey, Bob Ballard, George Cates, and Bob Smale. Joe Rizzo joined us back in the early fifties and has been a bulwark of strength in our arranging department. Joe does especially well with Latin American songs. He also plays bass fiddle and frequently does dates on his off nights.

Jack Pleis joined us to help rehearse the singers and to fit arrangements to them. His background as a pianist and recording director with RCA Victor is of great help to us.

Watching our Easter show take shape, I take great pride in the professionalism of all of our people. I pray that we may keep going for many years. There's a need for our kind of music to bridge the gap between the disco craze and classics.

Looking over our band and entertainers, I am reminded of former members and their impact on the Champagne Music Makers. The Lennon Sisters, JoAnn Castle, Pete Fountain, Clay Hart and Salli Flynn (now man and wife), Tanya Welk, Tiny Little, Lynn Anderson, Peanuts Hucko, Roberta Linn, Bill Page, Orie Amadeo, Dick Cathcart, and on and on. The passing parade. Each time someone left, two seemed to show up and take over.

"Yes, Lawrence, our cup is truly overflowing."

"If You Can't Play
the Melody...
Play Unison!"

I like to think of Lawrence Welk as the Arthur Fiedler of popular music—the Pied Piper of television. I can think of no one else who has done so much for music over such a sustained period of time. When I joined him in St. Louis in 1950, I could feel his total devotion to his audience and their tastes.

"They're our customers, you know," he always says. "If we don't please them, they'll go elsewhere for their music. And I wouldn't blame them!"

I, for one, owe a great debt of gratitude to Lawrence for his faith in me and for the many opportunities he has given me. I have learned much from this kind gentleman in terms of dedication, leadership, and musicianship; and the impact he has had on the entertainment world is the envy of many.

Members of the Welk musical family have a view of Lawrence that his TV audience is not able to enjoy. Through our togetherness in rehearsals, shows, and

207

travels, we have come to see this remarkable man much more closely than would otherwise be possible.

As most of his audiences know, Lawrence frequently apologizes for his lack of formal education. But to us who know him intimately, he need not apologize, for his background gives him a humility few people have. And this makes him a very human person. As a result, however, his enthusiasm is often way ahead of his words and this results in what members of the band, myself included, refer to as "Welkisms." And, being the humble human being that he is, Lawrence laughs at these along with the members of his musical family. They serve to lighten the precise scheduling and programming that is demanded of a successful show. As a matter of fact, we even wonder if Lawrence doesn't intentionally dream up these Welkisms for us to enjoy. Here are a few for you.

Art Depew, our trumpet man in the early sixties, was once late for our job at the Hollywood Palladium. "I'm sorry I'm late, boss," he said. "I just don't know what happened; I have no excuse."

"Art," Lawrence answered, "that's no excuse!"

The band was having an especially difficult rehearsal one day. Finally Lawrence heard one too many bad notes. He came out on the stage and said, "Boys, that's the last camel!"

Lawrence's trim and youthful appearance, despite his seventy-plus years, is ample evidence that he is very health-conscious. One day he spotted a delicious-looking lemon meringue pie in the cafeteria. His only comment (as I helped myself to a big piece), "I wouldn't eat that with a ten-foot pole!"

208

When the Air Force began testing the X-15 in California, Lawrence commented, "I hear there's been a lot of Masonic bombs around here lately."

Many years ago, a beautiful arrangement of "The Waters of the Minnetonka" was a very popular part of our concert schedule. We hadn't played it for a long time, though, when Lawrence decided, on the spur of the moment, to add it to a show we were doing at Indian Wells, California. Most of the band members at the show had never played the song and had no idea how it went. When Lawrence realized that no one could play his old favorite, he said, "If you can't play the melody, play unison!"

Our production staff has tried at various times to inject a little comedy into our show. After one such attempt, Lawrence scolded them, saying, "You have to realize that our show is ninety-five percent music, and only fifteen percent comedy!"

To Norman Bailey one night at the Aragon: "Not only are you playing the wrong notes, but I can't hear you!"

Bob Smale can be counted on to do something different every time he plays a number on the piano. He always astounds us with his instant command of any music. One evening the band gave him a big hand after an inspired rendition of "Body and Soul." Lawrence commented, "Bob, the boys tell me that you did a wonderful job on that, but it's not my cup of dish."

My solo one year at Harrah's Club in Lake Tahoe, Nevada, was "Dance of the Comedians." Lawrence and I were having trouble agreeing on the syncopation of one part of the melody, though we went over it again and again. Finally he said to me, "Wait here. I'll go get my barometer and show you what I mean."

Lawrence's comment about a politician who was being honored for some nice gesture: "That's a real feather in his head!"

Concerning the mass exodus of our senior citizen bus tour guests at two minutes past midnight, New Year's Eve at the Palladium: "The people left in *groves*."

To Jimmy Roberts, dressed in a raincoat and hat, waiting for his entrance cue for "Singing in the Rain": "Jimmy, you should not go out on stage dressed like that; people will think you were late and didn't care enough to change your clothes."

Cutting short a talkative salesman: "I need that like I need a hole in the ground!"

Introducing one of our featured band members: "Ladies and gentlemen, next we have a new member in our band, Alvin Ashby from Evansville, Indiana. Alvin, step up here and tell the people who you are and where you come from."

One of our new young female entertainers had a habit of being constantly late to rehearsal. Lawrence was aggravated, but reminded all of us, "We have to be patient and bend a little for her. She belongs to women's ad-lib."

Lawrence wanted a group picture at the opening of one of our TV shows. He said to Jim Hobson, our production manager: "Jim, give me a close-up of the entire band."

A few years ago, we were booked by the Shriners to play for one of their major functions. Lawrence was asked to introduce their Grand Potentate about halfway through the evening. He had a little trouble with that title, so he practiced it over and over till he had it down pat. Then he went out on the stage and said, "Ladies and gentlemen, may I introduce your Grand Totem Pole."

My first experience with Lawrence's unique accent occurred in St. Louis before I had actually joined the band. He used many sight gags during his shows, including horn-rim glasses with a false mustache and nose. One morning he mentioned that he had been looking all over for a "flat head." I didn't want to appear ignorant, and I was very anxious to please him, so I spent the entire next day looking for a "flat-head" for him. Nobody else had ever heard of one either, so at last, the next day, I confessed my failure. "No problem," he said, "I just flattened this one." And he showed me a black fedora hat he'd crumpled!

In 1966 Lawrence felt secure enough to think about building a new house for himself and Fern. He enlisted the services of a prominent architect and found a choice lot in Pacific Palisades. Soon the house was completed and it *was* "wunnerful!" It had an indoor swimming pool, putting green, pool table in the den, organ, and even a little bit of room set aside for an accordion.

As soon as he and Fern were settled, Lawrence invited the band members up for a little housewarming. Kenny Trimble and I, along with our wives, Bonnie and Berdyne, were among the first to arrive. Lawrence greeted us at the massive front door, saying proudly, "See what can happen when you just play the melody!"

After playing for President Eisenhower's inaugural ball, Lawrence and the whole band boarded a commercial airliner for the trip back to Hollywood. As it happened, the Guy Lombardo band was aboard that night also. As we were getting ready to land after a turbulent flight, the plane made a sudden steep climb—the pilot had discovered that, through some navigational error, he was headed right for the dirt *between* the runways and had to do some fancy maneuvering to get us back up to safety. Lawrence broke the tension of that sudden fright with, "Boy! If this plane goes down, Sammy Kaye will be an overnight sensation!"

Not long after that little close call, we came very near to a real disaster on a flight to Dallas. Our Electra prop-jet was tossed and buffeted about during a violent thunderstorm and battered by hurricane-force winds. Several times we were forced down to nearly treetop level as the pilots struggled to maintain control of the jet. I noticed that one of the younger stewardesses was crying, and most of the rest of us were paralyzed in our seats with fright—even *I*, the seasoned traveler, was turning into a "white-knuckle" flyer! When we finally came to a very rocky landing, Lawrence turned to me and said, "For a second there, I saw my whole life pass *between* my eyes!"

George Cates also comes up with a few good ones, for example: "I may not always be right. But I'm never wrong!"

Bill Daly, a friend and agent long associated with the band, is another lucky guy whose sense of humor is part original, and part "Welkism." He had adjusted to the loss of his left arm and handles himself as easily as those of us with two. In fact, he may do a little better:

> Lawrence was playing golf with Bill one sunny afternoon in Los Angeles. On the green Lawrence made a difficult fifteen-foot putt for a birdie. He turned to Bill and said, "Gee, I thought I'd get a little applause for that one!"
>
> Bill, who lost his left arm to a grenade in World War II, answered, "I *am* clapping, Lawrence!"

> Accosted by a mugger one night in Washington, D.C., Bill complied with the command, "Hands up!"
> "Both hands, fella," the mugger repeated.
> "Only got one!" Bill protested.
> "Well, then. *Hand* up!" the mugger answered— and then robbed him anyway.

Bill likes to tell about the year that he received only one cuff link from Joe Feeney for Christmas. A note was enclosed that he would receive the other one the following year. He did, too.

I'm sure that my close association with and great admiration for Lawrence over the years has caused me to pick up some of his habits—both the good ones *and* the funny ones. Let me relate one to you.

Bob Lido asked me to accompany him and a couple of the other members of the band to entertain at a home for unwed mothers many years ago. It was Christmastime, and the young women were a very appreciative audience. At the end of our impromptu show, I thanked them for inviting us and added, "I hope we see you all again next year!" I didn't remember where I was until they all started to laugh and shouted, "No! No!"

Now, one last Welkism that caused a loud response:

Introducing our beloved sponsor, the late Matthew Rosenhaus of the J.B. Williams Company, at Harrah's Club at Lake Tahoe one evening, Lawrence said, "Ladies and gentlemen, won't you welcome our good boss, Rosey Mattenhouse?"

Realizing his error, Lawrence added, "Oh dear. Maybe I should have stayed on the farm?"

As one, the audience and the Champagne Music Makers shouted, "No! No! No!"

And I couldn't agree more. The last thirty years have been great!

Bread upon the Waters

When I was a sophomore at Roslyn High School, an assembly speaker impressed me with his talk: "Success consists of rendering a service to the world."

Years later, while I waited in New York City for orders to depart for the ETO Camp Shows, I attended Norman Vincent Peale's Marble Collegiate Church one Sunday morning. Dr. Peale's inspiring sermon, "Love, the Greatest Feeling of All," made me think of what that speaker at Roslyn High had said. Both were talking about the same thing, though each put it differently: service is based on love, but love comes first.

How often in the midst of the daily round we forget that the single most important unit of the world is the individual—each member of our family, the neighbor next door, the person down the street. And we too often fail to remember that each individual, no matter how old, does have specific needs, not only for food and clothing and shelter, but for love, for the sure knowledge that there are others close by who offer security and strength through the sharing of joy and sorrow and concern.

In a nutshell, love is the essence of life, the basis of peace, the thing that binds us, one to another. It is the outward expression of the Golden Rule.

215

Looking back over my experience with music, I am reminded again and again that it is through music that I reach others with love. Back on the farm, Pa and Ma had their own particular ways of expressing love. They taught me that it can be shown in many different ways and through many different talents. So often I felt Pa's love as we sat watching the sunset without his saying a single word, or when he bundled us kids so warmly against the winter's cold before we set out in the horse-drawn sleigh. And Mother's love overflowed through her warm apple pies, through the patches she sewed to our worn clothes in the evening's dim light. In my own family there is a constant flow of love; it is there in the ways we speak and listen and in the many day-to-day things we do for each other. Often I think of how Pa read from the Bible, of his favorite passage from Corinthians: "There are but three things that last forever: faith, hope and love. But the greatest of these is love."

I think of my music as a sacred trust. I feel it is a trust of love and know that I am responsible for guarding it and nurturing it and using it to help others and to bring them joy. I believe God wants me to do this. He directed me to music when other interests were competing for my attention. He brought me through illnesses when doctors and family were afraid for my life. And when my heart was known to be a potential threat to health, He showed me the accordion, that thirty-five pound instrument that demands constant exercise and great strength of arms, shoulders, and chest muscles. Playing this instrument has made my heart strong, and has enabled me to fulfill my sacred trust.

And so I believe my mission in life is to reach out in love through music; I believe my accordion can send a prayer to God that He understands. I believe, too, that

216

others are healed and comforted through this musical prayer whether they listen, sing along, or meditate, for music reaches some deep and solitary place and allows the mind to open to receive God's blessing.

I came to understand this during the war, when I saw patients in seemingly hopeless straits respond by reaching out to life as my accordion spoke to them. I have seen soldiers, terribly frightened or deeply depressed, comforted and reawakened by the sound of music.

I remember one such incident in particular. It happened at an evacuation hospital in Germany. As I strolled through the wards playing a familiar hymn (I think it was "Beautiful Savior"), I heard a young soldier cry out. Thinking he was in terrible pain, I hesitated a moment, unsure whether or not I should continue. A lieutenant hurried to my side and whispered, "Please don't stop playing! That man hasn't made a sound in weeks; your music must have gotten through to him." A couple of hours later a chaplain told me he had spoken with the long-silent soldier after I left the ward. The chaplain said, "It seems the hymn you were playing was a favorite of that young man when he was a lad. He heard it, even in his deep coma. The doctors say it may very well have saved his life by rousing him and by giving him the will to live." Then he added, with a twinkle in his eye, "Now he won't stop talking!"

I often play for the residents of hospitals and convalescent centers. Whenever I do, I watch for that special light which shines from the faces of the elderly as they recognize a song full of memories. As they listen, they seem to feel alive and loved once again, and it shows as a kind of radiance that has a beauty all its own. It is not uncommon for a doctor to tell me that the music somehow touched a patient deeply and helped to dissolve depression or self-destructive thoughts. When I hear of such cases, I am

217

grateful to God for the talent He has given me, for the ability to reach out through love.

Captain Eddie Rickenbacker was one of my idols. Someone once asked him what was really important in life. He replied, "What you leave behind." It was not worldly possessions he was thinking of, it was the impact one makes on the lives of others—through some intangible good that lives on as a legacy for future generations.

Oscar Hammerstein said it a different way. Years ago, as actress Mary Martin waited to go onstage for the opening of one of Hammerstein's shows, she received a good-luck note from the gifted man himself. He had reached out from his deathbed to send a little verse he had written just for her. It ended with lines similar to these: "Love in your heart is not put there to stay. Love is not love till you give it away."

As an entertainer, I have always tried to give my audiences the feeling that they are the single most important part of my life while I am with them. Usually when I leave the stage, I am dripping wet from the effect of the show and from keeping the heavy accordion in constant motion. People worry that I give so much of myself that it will harm my health. It is not a worry for me, for I know that I *receive* much, much more from those who listen than I could ever give to them. And when I complete a show, I thank God for showing me the way to a career in music, for it is His love for me that has allowed me to dispense love to others through music.

Yes, I am constantly reminded that in the final analysis, the one who gives love is the one who receives it. My bread has returned many times.

Epilogue

As I was working on the final chapters of this book, I had a four-day tour starting in Beloit, Wisconsin, proceeding to Pennsylvania, South Dakota, and finishing in Missouri. I flew into Chicago, rented a car and drove to Beloit. My accordion could not fit in the trunk; so it rode on the back seat.

It was raining when I checked in at the motel; so I parked the car outside my room and went inside to check things out before returning for my luggage.

My suitcase and suit bag went in first along with a heavy box of music. Then I went back for the accordion.

The car was empty! No accordion! My favorite instrument was gone!

I had nursed the reeds in this instrument for 15 years, keeping the old reeds when I'd get a new accordion. Worst of all, the show was two and a half hours away! Where would I get an accordion?

I called the manager, who in turn called the police. In less than 15 minutes the theft was on police radio and the Beloit radio stations.

The manager located another accordion for the show, but no other instrument plays like your own. To say that I was devastated would be the understatement of the year.

It was as though a good and true friend had died in sudden tragedy.

I phoned Berdyne, who can usually cheer me up in my low moments, but she finally gave up.

I arrived back in Los Angeles on Monday morning to find that Faithe Deffner had sent a new Pancordion for me to use, but it still wasn't my old "friend."

When I called Berdyne to tell her I was on the ground, she said, "Better call Sam Lutz right away. He says some lady in Wisconsin claims she has your accordion."

Wonder of wonders!

I called Peg Nelson at her guitar studio in Beloit. Yes, she was sure she had my accordion. I asked, "Does it have a little hole near the top of the strap?" "Yes." "And some extra screws in the top of the bass side?" "Yes." "Does it look a little beat up?" "Yes. And it looks very lonesome," she said.

"That's my accordion," I said. "God bless you for your goodness and honesty."

"When I found out that it belonged to you, I thought of all the shut-ins and handicaps you have entertained, and how important it is that this be returned to you."

"I'll be in Washington, Iowa, next Thursday. You could ship it to Cedar Rapids, and I'll pick it up at the airport."

"In the meantime," she said, "I'll leave it with the nuns at Our Lady of Assumption Convent where it will be safe."

"By the way," I asked, "How much did you have to pay for the accordion?"

"Sixty dollars," was her answer. For an accordion worth thousands!

Now *that* really upset me!!